WESTFIELD PUBLICATIONS IN MEDIEVAL STUDIES

Essays on Thomas Hoccleve

WESTFIELD PUBLICATIONS
IN
MEDIEVAL STUDIES

Volume 10

CENTRE FOR MEDIEVAL
AND RENAISSANCE STUDIES
QUEEN MARY AND WESTFIELD COLLEGE
UNIVERSITY OF LONDON
1996

Essays on Thomas Hoccleve

Edited by Catherine Batt

CENTRE FOR MEDIEVAL
AND RENAISSANCE STUDIES
QUEEN MARY AND WESTFIELD COLLEGE
UNIVERSITY OF LONDON
1996

BREPOLS

© 1996 ⊜ BREPOLS
Printed in Belgium
D/1996/0095/24
ISBN 2-503-85404-X

Contents

Contributors

CATHERINE Batt has taught at Birkbeck College, Queen Mary and Westfield College, and Royal Holloway College, University of London, and at the University of Durham, and is now a Lecturer in the School of English at the University of Leeds. She has published on Clemence of Barking, the *Gawain*-Poet, Malory, and Caxton.

Charles Blyth is a graduate of Harvard, an independent scholar who has published a major study of Gavin Douglas' *Aeneid*, and whose work has appeared in *Philological Quarterly*, the *Chaucer Review*, *Essays in Criticism*, and *Speculum*. He is currently preparing an edition of *The Regiment of Princes*.

Roger Ellis is a Senior Lecturer in the School of English Studies, Communication and Philosophy at the University of Wales College of Cardiff. He has worked on late medieval religious writing, including the religious narratives of Chaucer, and the *Revelations* of St Bridget of Sweden, and organizes a biennial conference on medieval translation. He is editing a selection of Hoccleve's poetry, to include the *Series,* for Dent Everyman.

David Mills is a Professor in the Department of English Language and Literature at the University of Liverpool. His published work includes articles on Langland and the *Gawain*-Poet and a major contribution to Volume I of *The Revels History of Drama in English*. He has co-edited the standard edition of the *Chester Mystery Cycle*, and, with Elizabeth Baldwin, is currently editing the Cheshire records for the *Records of Early English Drama*.

Acknowledgements

THESE essays developed from or grew out of interest in a day conference on 'Hoccleve and Fifteenth-century Writings' held at the Centre for English Studies, Senate House, University of London, in March 1994. I wish to thank everyone who took part in the conference, whether as contributors of papers, or participants in other capacities, and especially Dr Warren Chernaik, Director of the Centre for English Studies, University of London, and Ms Greta Cerasale, Secretary, for the support and administrative help that made the conference possible. I wish also to thank those at Queen Mary and Westfield College, University of London, whose expertise, advice and goodwill have been invaluable in the production of this book: Professor Alan Deyermond, General Editor of the Westfield Publications in Medieval Studies series, Centre for Medieval and Renaissance Studies, Ms Rosamund Allen, Director of the Centre for Medieval and Renaissance Studies, and Brian Place, Arts Computing Manager.

INTRODUCTION

Catherine Batt

'ffreend, looth me were nay seye vn-to yow,
But y suppose / it may noon othir be,
Lest wommen vn-to Magge, the good kow,
Me likne / and thus seye / "o, beholde & see
The double man / o, yondir, lo, gooth he
That hony first yaf / and now yeueth galle:
He fo in herte is / vn-to wommen alle"'.[1]

   In these lines from the Prologue to the story of *Jonathas*,
part of the sequence of interconnected narratives and accounts
of the production of those narratives that modern readers
know as the *Series*, the Hoccleve persona remonstrates with
his Friend who, having recommended that he write a work
extolling women (*Dialogue* 743–91), as a penance for his

---

[1] *Jonathas: Prologue*, ed. Furnivall (1970), ll. 36–41. Following the
author-date system, reference to texts will give the date of the latest revision
of Furnivall's edition, by Doyle and Mitchell (see the bibliography for
details of publication). Reference to Furnivall's critical apparatus, however,
will be to the original date of publication (1892). Future references to the
Series are by line number, in the text.

having insulted them, or being thought to have done so, in an earlier poem, is now asking him to rework another story, that of *Jonathas*, in order to warn the Friend's young son against women's wiles. The Friend reassures the Narrator that the story's moral exigency will cancel out any perception of its author as duplicitous: 'vnhonest wommen' (63) are legitimately open to opprobrium and censure. Hoccleve consents to write the tale and so the pragmatically structured *Series* continues to grow.

Hoccleve's alarm about sending out conflicting signals that might have an adverse effect on how others perceive him as a private individual gains extra poignancy from his declared personal situation. From the opening *Complaint* onwards, he is struggling against a general perception quick to interpret any inconsistency of character as evidence of the continuation of a depressive illness from which he no longer suffers. As James Simpson has recently observed, Hoccleve is especially anxious to convince others that he is now stable, and that his narrating voice should be regarded as such (1991, 21). In the earlier *Dialogue*, he has already found a certain self-assurance, in his claim that no-one can presume completely to know another (477–83). For Simpson, this latter assertion confirms that element of privacy integral to the audience-author relationship (1991, 26). However, the above lines expose the degree to which extant social and literary practices institutionalize narratorial inconsistency: the Friend who is concerned about the stability of Hoccleve's private self and demands continuity of it, is paradoxically insouciant about disjunctions in narratorial presentation that themselves help to constitute the Hoccleve persona. At the same time, Hoccleve's anxiety emphasizes the difficulty, on the part of writer as of reader, of drawing boundaries between author and text, of separating the narrator from the private individual, especially when such a large part of that text concerns itself with Hoccleve as fictive subject.

The 'doubleness' that Hoccleve advertises here and elsewhere, his acute perception of literature as a continual and potentially contradictory play of assumptions, expectations and subjective interests, on a social as on a literary plane, seems at odds with the straightforward, even transparent, individual a modern critical assessment has confidently extrapolated from his writings. F.J. Furnivall, his nineteenth-century editor, describes him as a 'weak, sensitive, look-on-the-worst side kind of man' (1892, xxxviii): nearly a century later, Malcolm Richardson is inveighing against an incompetent bureaucrat who is 'a bungler, misfit, and perpetual also-ran' (1985-86, 321). These judgements of course immediately provoke contradiction from other internal evidence, but the eagerness with which some interpret an aspect of the literary persona so literally must derive at least in part from the minutely-realized, apparently historically corroborated, social and personal life with which Hoccleve presents us in his fictions.

But if Hoccleve's very method encourages us to relate, as seamlessly as possible, a textually-constructed self to a socially-formed individual, his writings also, as many recognize, conflate social, political and poetical concerns in such a way as to make us pay closer attention to what Paul Strohm, writing about fourteenth-century literature, has characterized as a text's 'social imagination' (1992). In doing so, we quickly appreciate how difficult it is to distinguish between strata of social and textual in any attempt to gauge the nature of Hoccleve's work. To assess the impact of these writings, we have then to try to reconstitute, not only (insofar as is possible) separate areas of inquiry — for example, the importance of certain kinds of literary allusion in vernacular literature, or the status of the government post Hoccleve occupied — but the quality of the interaction of these elements, the significance of collapsing the interests and rhetoric of one area into another.

At the day conference at which earlier versions of three of the essays here were presented, the business of literary and historical reconstruction and contextualization was a central concern, though it manifested itself in a variety of critical approaches. Papers from John Burrow and Lee Patterson (neither of which features here) offered a frame for the conference which illustrated the range of means by which modern scholars might recuperate and interpret the historical in relation to Hoccleve. John Burrow had just completed his life of Thomas Hoccleve for the Variorum press (1994), in which he gathers together the documentation still available on the clerk of the Privy Seal. His talk, which opened the conference, stressed the importance of material witness with, as an example, discussion of a document, PRO E 28/9, a memorandum of proceedings of the King's Council, 23 July 1401 (and reproduced in Burrow [1994, 35–36]). The document is both a petition to the Council on the part of eight Privy Seal clerks, Hoccleve among them, for some financial compensation for the increase in workload their office has had to bear in the recent past, and a record of the grant of forty pounds made to them in response to this request. Conventionally 'literary' evidence can help to place Hoccleve's text: for example, what are at first sight near-anachronistic expressions of individuality, quasi-modern concerns with representations of the self, may turn out, as Eva Thornley shows, to be commonplaces of the penitential mode (1967). Similarly, Burrow's presentation of the biographical evidence, which combines consideration of Hoccleve's petitionary poems and of the government documents in which he makes request for payment, among other things confirms, from the 'historical' evidence, that the clerk characterized as an idiosyncratic constant complainer is simply ensuring that he is paid what he is owed, in the register acceptable for phrasing such demands.

As Patterson demonstrated through his conference paper's outline of recent trends in Hoccleve studies, there is no firm concensus on Hoccleve's importance, either as a Privy Seal clerk or as a writer. While a deal of material concerning the poet is extant, it still leaves open to speculation issues of basic interest to those of us interested in literary and cultural contexts: what, for example, is the precise nature of Hoccleve's political allegiance? Is he writing primarily for the Lancastrian regime, or is he an 'independent' poet? And what of the status of court culture at the time, and the nature of Hoccleve's position within such a culture: is it in fact possible to speak of court culture as homogeneous in the early fifteenth century? The details of Hoccleve's life are fuller than those available for many medieval writers, and Burrow is able to supply a chronology for Hoccleve by which he is born c. 1367, joins the Privy Seal office in (possibly) 1387, and dies between March and May 1426, after many years in government service (1994, 32). But just as the evidence suggests a potential, if not an exactly-quantifiable, ambivalence attaching to Hoccleve's social position,[2] so it is not possible to be precise about his status as a writer. There is some debate, for example, over the truth or extent of his claimed acquaintance with Chaucer, to whom Hoccleve assigns the roles of both teacher and parent in *The Regiment of Princes*, and Burrow supplies a measured overview of

---

[2] M.C. Seymour sees his position as ambiguous:

An educated man yet not a graduate, in close contact with the rich and influential yet not gentle-born nor of independent means, the medieval government clerk must always have moved uneasily between the two classes of society. (1981, 117)

Pearsall cites Seymour with some approval (1994, 394), but is also more positive about the kind of access to the upper echelons of society Hoccleve's work would have afforded him.

critical opinion on this issue (1994, 10–11). Meanwhile, David Lawton argues, from evidence of Hoccleve's experience as a copyist of literary works, a privileged position for the government official as one of Chaucer's first editors, and postulates (on grounds primarily of theme and style) that he might have been responsible for writing some of the linking stanzas within the *Canterbury Tales* (1985, 27–29).

Certainly, the broader evidence of manuscript and early print shows Hoccleve's work could feature both as commentary on, or within collections of, Chaucer's productions and Chaucer-related literature. Oxford, Christ Church MS 152, a copy of the *Canterbury Tales*, assigns the younger poet's *Miracle of the Virgin* to one of Chaucer's pilgrims, as *The Ploughman's Tale*, fols 228b–231a (ed. Bowers 1992, 23–32). The *Letter of Cupid* (1402) is an example of how Hoccleve's poetry circulated in a range of contextualizations. Printers such as William Thynne publish this poem as Chaucer's own work (Burrow 1994, 54), while in the mid fifteenth-century Durham, University Library MS Cosin V.ii.13, it appears as a 'companion-piece' to *Troilus and Criseyde* (Piper, 1989). The *Letter* also appears in an anthology of court poetry extant as Oxford, Bodleian Library MS Tanner 346, assembled in the 1440s, and including Lydgate's *Temple of Glas*, and the F-Prologue to Chaucer's *Legend of Good Women*: Seth Lerer has analysed this group of texts as a highly self-conscious collection of discourses of love that also addresses questions about the production, patronage and reception of love poetry (1993, 60–72). The most cursory look at some of the different means of circulation of one text suggests then that Hoccleve is working within a culture that exercises a sophisticated range of responses to texts and textuality: from the information of the written evidence we clearly need to be more open and flexible about ideas of literary authority, the autonomy of the text, and authorial status.

Correlative to his interest in the relation between text, author and reader, which reflects contemporary attitudes towards the written, is the care Hoccleve evidently took over the manuscript production of his own work. There are arguments that those collections of short pieces that survive, in Hoccleve's hand, as San Marino, CA, Huntington Library MSS HM 111 and HM 744, are very consciously organized by the poet as works of self-promotion.[3] Other holograph manuscripts are extant; a copy of the *Series*, now Durham, University Library MS Cosin V.iii.9, is dedicated to the Countess of Westmorland, and the huge *Formulary*, now British Library MS Additional 24062, evidence of Hoccleve's meticulousness as a civil servant, gives documentary record, in the form of 'model' pieces in French and Latin, of the kind of work his office undertook (Burrow 1994, 4–5).

Hoccleve's care, however, and with it his reputation for technical accomplishment as a poet, have not been best served by his nineteenth-century editor, whose whimsical approach is famously illustrated in a brief report on the Hammersmith Girls' Sculling Club and notes on the delights of a country summer ('bother Hoccleve!' [1897, xx]), offered in *lieu* of an adequate preface to his edition of the *Regiment of Princes*, a poem the proper editing of which Furnivall at least has the grace to acknowledge is 'work that needs effort' (1897, xix). Charles Blyth, who has taken over from David Greetham the task of editing the *Regiment of Princes*, touches, in his article on this project, on some of the shortcomings of Furnivall's edition of London, British Library MS Harley 4866. Blyth's own project looks at the evidence from this manuscript, evidently a presentation copy the production of which

---

[3] See Bowers (1989a), and John Burrow's brief but to-the-point review of critical assessments of the manuscripts and what they reveal about Hoccleve's practice (1994, 31).

Hoccleve may well have supervised, and at the other surviving presentation copy, now British Library MS Arundel 38.[4] There is no holograph manuscript of the *Regiment*, but Blyth draws on the wealth of evidence that exists from other contexts to establish aspects of Hoccleve's authorial practice, presenting examples to justify his method in the preparation of what he readily describes as (like any edition) a work of reconstruction and interpretation. With the new edition of the *Regiment*, and editions of the *Series* now in progress (among them Roger Ellis' project for Dent Everyman), complete versions of Hoccleve's texts will be made more accessible, and to a broader range of readers.

The recent edition of *Poems of Cupid, God of Love*, by Fenster and Erler (1990) in which the *Letter of Cupid* appears, brings the English poem together with the French work from which it derives, the *Epistre au Dieu d'Amours* by Christine de Pizan, and allows one readily to see how this early poem enters into dialogue with the text on which it depends. In his article, 'Chaucer, Christine de Pizan, and Hoccleve: *The Letter of Cupid*', Roger Ellis analyses that dialogue, and draws out the ways in which Hoccleve's poem now endorses, now offers a critique of, the values and tone of the original. Ellis, with his suggestion that Christine knew and used Chaucer's works, traces a more complex cultural exchange between French and English poetry than is usually acknowledged, and demonstrates too how Hoccleve employs Chaucer to inform

---

[4] For a description of these manuscripts, see Seymour (1974, 263–64, 269). Seymour speculates that the Harley MS was perhaps the one Hoccleve is known to have presented to Edward, Duke of York, or John, Duke of Bedford (1974, 169), though see also Burrow (1994, 23) on whether Edward in fact was given a copy of the *Regiment*. That Hoccleve appears to have had the means to produce at least three de-luxe presentation copies of his poem is part of the contradictory evidence surrounding his proclaimed poverty (Simpson 1995, 150, n. 2).

his own reading of Christine. Hoccleve emerges here as greatly concerned with the nature and potential of court style: but while he exposes the dangers, inherent in Christine's original, of refuting antifeminist discourse on its own terms, the poem itself, Ellis suggests, doesn't ultimately resolve all the contradictions of the *Epistre*. Ellis characterizes the poem as an exercise in tightrope walking, and one could extend this observation to many of Hoccleve's poems: Hoccleve seems above all interested in balancing several meanings simultaneously. In doing so, he stretches to the limit the interpretative possibilities language offers.

This interest in testing the boundaries of register and genre perhaps accounts for why Hoccleve so often locates his persona either outside, or on the margins of, social and literary institutions and frameworks, as a means of presenting afresh to us familiar genres, whether of advice literature (as in the *Regiment*) or (for example, in the *Series*), of treatises on mortality; he thus both tries the limits of modes of representation and exercises a certain metatextual control over them. David Mills' article, 'The Voices of Thomas Hoccleve', presents a nuanced analysis of how books and voices inform one another in the *Series* and how Hoccleve dramatizes the dynamic of literary exchange so as to make registers comment one upon the other. The destabilizing effect of a reader's intervention in the writing process is well-documented as a central structuring fiction in the *Series*, but at the same time, inscribed in the whole project is a shrewd awareness of how these texts do not escape the contingencies of actual patronage — the book he says he is producing for Duke Humphrey (*Dialogue* 526–46) and the sequence sent to Joan Beaufort, Countess of Westmorland (who, as John of Gaunt's daughter by Katherine Swynford, is half-aunt to Humphrey, Duke of Gloucester), are perhaps not the same text, at least in terms of their reception. While, then, Hoccleve comments self-reflexively on literary production in his poetry, he also places it firmly within a historical context, but in such a way as recognizes the provisionality of his hold as author upon his own material, and the variability of reader response.

David Lawton, in his important article on 'Dullness and the Fifteenth Century', suggests that Chaucer's literary successors seek to make their work politically relevant where Chaucer himself playfully claims for his texts 'a space for fiction that is apart from the public world of truth' (1987, 762). My own essay in this volume posits a Chaucer more overtly politically aware of the power and nature of language and I therefore see a greater continuity between the earlier poet and Hoccleve. I consider how we might try to evaluate the political force of court literature, primarily by means of an examination and contextualization of the interpretative difficulties posed by a highly rhetorical passage in the *Regiment* which appears to be written in defence of women: I argue especially from what I understand as this passage's debt to Chaucer that it makes us acutely aware of the relation between language, perception and society and that such awareness does not necessarily seek to confirm the policies of the crown, but claims consideration in its own right in the world of political decision-making and responsibility.

In their different ways the articles here all argue for a reconsideration of a range of Hoccleve's texts as works of some complexity and subtlety, within a cultural context the nuances of which we are only beginning to recuperate and appreciate. There has been a welcome increase in interest in Hoccleve studies in recent years, not least in the areas of patronage, and the dynamics and conditions of literary production, engagement and response, and the relation of vernacular literature to political power (Scanlon 1994). This volume is a small contribution to what will, one hopes, prove a continuing and fruitful process of recovery and appreciation.

Editing *The Regiment of Princes*

Charles Blyth

THE need for a new edition of Hoccleve's *Regiment of Princes* is evident when one reflects on the date of the last edition (1897) and the identity of its editor.[1] In addition, the considerable amount of attention paid to Hoccleve in the past fifteen years or so suggests the appropriateness of an edition more responsive to current scholarly interests and practice. Though some have chided Furnivall for basing his text on British Library, MS Harley 4866 primarily for its superior Chaucer portrait, Harley is, of the 43 surviving manuscripts, one of only two patronal copies (the other is BL MS Arundel 38). It is thus not a bad choice for a base manuscript and, given the speed with which he must have worked, Furnivall is not a careless transcriber. Nonetheless, his text is more like a rough approximation of a diplomatic edition than a critical one. Furnivall fails to correct some evident errors in the manuscript and introduces a few errors of his own. He injects annoying, sometimes misleading, punctuation and orthographic

---

[1] F.J. Furnivall (1897). References to this edition are by line number in the text.

flourishes such that the pleasure of this edition ends with its marvellous Forewords. Finally, Furnivall isn't a very good reader of Hoccleve. One of the unexpected developments in recent fifteenth-century studies has been the upward reappraisal of Hoccleve's poetry — by, for example, such critics as A.C. Spearing and John Burrow. But Furnivall had no very good sense of Hoccleve's prosody, and the text he produced can only give encouragement to the old view that Hoccleve, whatever the interest of his passages of autobiography, was a pretty worthless versifier. Therefore one major goal of the new edition of the *Regiment* will be to present a text less subject to the charge of 'wanton accentuation' and 'jolting verse' — the charges of G. Gregory Smith writing shortly after the edition appeared (1900, 18).

There are very few outright errors, as when Furnivall at line 2286 has Marcus Regulus praised for resisting 'unknyghtly *trikkes*', a noun occurring neither in Harley nor in any of the other manuscripts. Harley and the majority read 'tukkes' or close variants thereof, of difficult origin but probably a variant of 'tacches'. But such errors as there are much more typically come from the manuscripts, not from the editor. Thus Furnivall's text for line 7 reads: 'Thought me bereft of sleep with force and myght'. A footnote indicates that the other manuscript Furnivall consults, British Library, MS Royal 17.D.vi, reads 'the' for 'with', but the leaf with Harley's original text is wanting. It is replaced by a modern hand which copies closely from another *Regiment* manuscript, that at the Rosenbach Museum & Library, and the Rosenbach text is the only one to give the reading 'with'.[2]

---

[2] A brief listing of all the MSS together with a graphic depiction of their affiliation is provided in Greetham (1987, 66–67). For additional notes on the connection between BL MS Harley 4866 and Philadelphia, PA, Rosenbach Museum & Library MS 1083/30, see A.S.G. Edwards (1993).

Or consider the garbled lines in Furnivall's text, in which the Old Man of the prologue warns Hoccleve of the dangers of solitariness:

'Whil þou art soulë, þoght is wastyng seed,
Swich in þe, & þat in grete foysoun,
And þou redeles, nat canst voyde his poysoun.' (201–3)

While a couple of the worst manuscripts expand 'is' to 'is a' (anxiety is a wasting seed), consultation of the manuscripts and common sense remind one that 'is' is a variant spelling of 'his'. The larger problem comes with the next line ('Swich/Swyche' in Arundel and Harley), which in other manuscripts is variously written 'such', or extended to 'suche is', or replaced with 'See I' or 'Which is'. The source of the problem is one of the most commonplace ambiguities in medieval paleography, the resemblance of lower-case 'c' to lower case 't', coupled with the possibility of omitting the vowel between two consonants (here 'o' betweeen 's' and 'w'). Furnivall doesn't help the sense by adding a comma at the end of the first line. On inspection, it is clear that the second line completes the figure of speech introduced in the preceding line: 'While you are alone, Anxiety sows his wasting seed in you and [does so] abundantly, so that, without counsel, you can't eject his poison'. Evidently the scribes here were copying line by line without attending to the context of syntax and figurative language — here a figure which A.C. Spearing has identified as a distinctive feature of Hoccleve's style. Spearing writes of Hoccleve's 'persistent use of small-scale personification' as 'one of the hallmarks of his style throughout his work' (1985, 119). In this case many of the scribes missed this hallmark. Awareness of the nonsense of the lines as presented, among others, by Arundel and Harley, combined with rudimentary familiarity with medieval handwriting, identify the error without external recourse. But in this case two identifiable groups of later scribal copies, one generally very good, the other often inferior, give the correct reading.

A new edition of the *Regiment* would necessarily correct these errors of the old edition, and it would do so in part by making use of the evidence provided by manuscripts which Furnivall did not consult. However, before turning to other desiderata of the edition, it is important to put down reasons for not simply replacing Furnivall's largely variation-free text with one meticulously providing the historical collation of all 43 manuscripts. It is true that M.C. Seymour, the originator of this project, in a note to his excellent edition of Hoccleve *Selections*, advises that 'a full collation of all manuscripts will appear in the forthcoming critical edition of the *Regiment of Princes*' (1981, xxxv). However, having completed that full collation, I maintain that such full disclosure would offer a mass of data, most of it of little or no value in establishing a critical text, in addition to entailing a wasteful, costly amount of space. For instance, less than a decade ago, the Early English Text Society published an edition of *The Pilgrimage of the Lyfe of the Manhode* — the anonymous fifteenth-century prose translation of the Deguileville poem (ed. Henry 1985–88). The work survives in six manuscripts. The text of the edition takes up 175 pages; the variants fill 181 pages of very small type. If you converted Furnivall's *Regiment* text to prose the type-size of the Deguileville text, it would fill 75–80 pages. Were the variations in all 43 manuscripts to be recorded, you would be talking (conservatively) about over 500 pages — of course exclusive of text, introduction, glossary, and explanatory notes. In recognition of the economic problem, some have suggested that such data could be provided on microfiches (Professor Burrow has suggested a Kangaroo Hoccleve with pouch), and recent developments in computer editions suggest alternative modes of non-print publication.

However, there has to be an intellectual justification for 'full disclosure': if it is important, it belongs in the book; if it isn't, it shouldn't be there at all. For the very few individuals who seek data on how 43 scribes altered the text, almost always in trivial ways, often merely by way of spelling variation, this editor would be happy to supply xeroxed collation sheets. But the very nature of the textual transmisson of the *Regiment* suggests why such data should not encumber the edition itself. Utterly unlike the situation of the B-text of *Piers Plowman*, or indeed any of the texts of *Piers Plowman*, we have, as already noted, two patronal copies, made with the probable though unprovable supervision of the poet, which have a degree of authority rare in Middle English writing. Apart from a quite small number of errors of the sort I've illustrated, these manuscripts are excellent; in particular, MS Arundel 38 is uncommonly careful, incorporating several neatly-made corrections by the scribe. Furthermore, even in the 41 non-patronal copies, especially if we eliminate the five or six worst offenders, the amount of significant substantive variation is quite small. Any one of half a dozen of these manuscripts would make a very good copy-text if we didn't have the even better patronal copies. In the absence of much substantive variation, it strikes me that the comprehensive recording of variations that depart from well-attested, demonstrably original readings is an exercise in pedantic waste.

I do not deny the interest or importance of many of the scribal copies. For instance, to cite two of the very worst from a textual standpoint, there is Cambridge, Corpus Christi College MS 496, in which we have the name of the Clare College student who, in copying the text in the 1440s, chose to leave out the poem's longest exemplum, the story of John of Canace, because, he says, it is of no value. Or there is Cambridge, University Library MS Hh.iv.11 which, though the smallest in size and one of the crudest in text and script, has the largest quantity of pictorial ornament of any manuscript, including its profusion of banderoles containing catchy rhyming proverbs in English.

Then, too, there is the cultural context provided by those manuscripts which group the *Regiment* together with other works (London, Society of Antiquaries MS 134; BL MS Harley 7333), or the five manuscripts which group it with Hoccleve's *Series* poems. However, unlike what Ralph Hanna has recently reported about the complex transmission of Trevisa's translation of the *Polychronicon* (1992, 112–20), the surviving manuscripts of the *Regiment* witness to no diverse textual tradition, and so have little bearing on establishing a critical text of the poem. What one can learn from such manuscripts belongs in separate studies of the poem and its context, not in the apparatus of an edition.

Thus the edition frankly privileges the two relatively 'authorized' manuscripts and corrects them where they evidently err. Recourse to other readings can serve to confirm one's sense of error, and in some cases doubtless facilitates the recognition of probable error. However, the reason for emending 'swich' to 'sowith' in the example given above is that the first word makes no sense in this context and contains the cause of its error, not because a given number of other manuscripts support another reading.

The third reason for rejecting 'full disclosure' returns me to discussing what the new edition *will* entail: its unconventional use of an additional authority in the form of the Hoccleve holographs. Over twenty years ago Seymour, in the preface to the first volume of the edition of Trevisa's *On the Properties of Things*, of which he was also the general editor, in a footnote remarked that '[t]he necessary procedures' for recovering 'much of Trevisa's spelling habits' are 'tested, in a forthcoming edition, on Hoccleve's *Regiment of Princes* against the extant holographs of his minor poems' (1975, Vol. 1: xii, n. 1). Nothing came of Seymour's forecast until, nearly a decade later, David Greetham, who replaced Seymour as General Editor of the *Regiment*, after initially taking a traditional approach to editing the poem, presented a concerted defence and methodology for an edition of the non-holograph *Regiment* making use of the authorial spellings recoverable from the holographs. Greetham published two papers on the subject (1985, 1987), and began supervising the preparation of a text by a team of editors to which I was a fairly late addition. Without Greetham's work, this edition would not be taking anything like its present form. Nor would I be carrying it out in this form if I did not largely agree with Greetham's argument. However, I depart from him in my sense of why the use of the holographs is not only possible but necessary. And at the same time, two historical problems which Greetham didn't address create complications and so call for additional arguments by way of defence. If these arguments are accepted, I believe they support my decision in this edition to give priority to the evidence supplied by the Hoccleve holographs and the patronal copies of the *Regiment*, and correspondingly less attention to historical collation.

Apart from its extended description of computer-assisted procedures for recovering holograph usage, the main interest of Greetham's earlier essay (1985) is its argument for resorting to such procedures. Greetham begins by noting a broad general distinction between editions of early texts (classical and medieval) which are typically concerned with reconstructing the archetype of extant manuscripts, and thus involved with the genealogy of texts, often employing Lachmannian stemmatics; and editions of post-Gutenberg texts, in which considerable attention is paid not merely to substantives but to accidentals — that is, to authorial preference in spelling, punctuation, and the like. Hoccleve's *Regiment of Princes* then is offered to test the possibility of combining in one edition a classical, Lachmannian construction of the poem's substantive readings, with a reconstruction of authorial accidentals which goes beyond those of the archetype (the antecedent of the early Arundel and Harley manuscripts) to authorial practice as revealed in the holographs.

For Greetham the main object of the edition was to produce an exemplary illustration of how one could merge these seemingly opposed traditions of editorial practice. He felt that there would be little value deriving from a new edition of the *Regiment* which merely improved on Furnivall by correcting errors and removing Furnivall's annoying practices, and drawing on a larger repertoire of scribal manuscripts. Though intrigued by Greetham's theoretical project, the more time I spent studying the holographs, the more I came to recognize other, quite practical, and also compelling, reasons for applying holograph forms to the *Regiment* text than Greetham's planned solution to a theoretical problem.

The Hoccleve holographs provide a rare opportunity to witness a medieval English poet writing out his own verse. That is a novel situation, as Seymour and Greetham recognized: somehow, one intuitively feels, the holographs must help us in gaining access to authorial intention; yet one knows that there are illusions and dangers in the territory of authorial intention, and one needs to take a hard look at what is involved in negotiating that territory.

While the desirability of approximating authorial usage has often been cited by editors — usually in the context of selecting a copy text judged to come closest to that usage — it isn't often that authorial practice is readily recoverable, and from that standpoint the Hoccleve holographs permit an unusually felicitous, seemingly unproblematic, use. For, apart from the *Formulary* Hoccleve made at the end of his life (almost all texts in Latin or French) and a few prose passages in the Durham manuscript, the holographs are in verse, so one isn't attempting to apply the language of a will or of a body of personal letters to the editing of a poem. Furthermore, it is highly compatible verse. Apart from a group of religious poems, there is remarkable overlap between the poetry of the holographs and that of the *Regiment* — passages in Hoccleve's autobiographical mode, passages of social and political observation, passages of moral instruction. At the more local level, the *Regiment* is written, but for its short envoi, entirely in rhyme royal; nearly all of the poems in the holograph are either in rhyme royal or in the 8-line stanza of Chaucer's *Monk's Tale*. Moving to the still more local level, the holographs exhibit a high degree of regularity in two areas: in habits of spelling, and in metrical practice. In both areas it is possible to establish Hocclevean patterns of usage.

Though by modern standards Hoccleve is not a consistent speller, by the standards of his time — by comparison, say, with any of the 43 scribes copying the *Regiment* — he is an exceptionally regular speller. The great majority of words in his lexicon have a single spelling. 'Thow' and 'yow' are always spelt that way, never 'thou' or 'you'. The past tense of the verb 'to think' is always, all 33 times, spelt 'thoghte', clearly distinguishing it from the spelling without 'e' which indicates either the noun (21 times) or the past participle (5 times). There is plainly no complication in transferring such spellings to the forms which appear in the scribal Arundel. In addition, there is a large percentage of common words which are spelt the same in the holographs and in Arundel and/or Harley, so that scribal form duplicates authorial form. That leaves two problematic categories of words: those for which there is more than a single holograph spelling, and those words in the *Regiment* that don't occur in the holographs. In the first category, we have, for example, 'deeth' (124 times), spelt with double 'e', against 'deth' with single 'e' (twice) — with no justification such as rhyme position. The exception is scarcely worrisome, and we can speak confidently of a preferred spelling. But then there are cases such as the spelling of the noun 'estat' with one 'a', in non-rhyme position, twice, against 'estaat' with double 'a', in non-rhyme position, three times — where one can't certainly identify a single Hocclevean form. A handful of words have as many as three spellings. However, provided that these variations are recognized and made use of, rather than regularized out of existence, in the 'translation' from scribal form to holograph form, I don't see a problem. The fact that there is not 100% regularity in Hoccleve's spelling habits does not mean that we can't make use of such regularity as there is.

As to the second category of words in the *Regiment* that are not present at all in the holographs, most can be reconstructed by analogy to holograph forms. For instance, the first line of the *Regiment* contains the adjective 'restless'. The holographs have the noun 'reste' (10 occurrences). And they also have the suffix '-less' attached to other nouns: 51 times spelt with double vowel ('-lees'), twice (again the minor variant) with single vowel ('-les'). Thus we construct a form beginning 'rest-' and ending '-lees'. But will there be an 'e' in the middle? There is a definite answer, provided by analogy from the holographs, and it points ahead to what will occupy much of the last part of this paper. The structurally similar word 'comfortless' occurs twice in the holographs, but in two distinct spellings: 'confortlees' and 'confortelees'. Nor is there anything capricious about the variation here. The metrical pattern calls for a three-syllable word in one case and a four-syllable word in the other. In the first line of the *Regiment*, we need two-syllable 'restlees', not three-syllable 'restelees'. Thus access to the holographs and the principle of analogy delivers the word 'restlees', which in this case happens to be the spelling the Arundel scribe uses. But even though I use Arundel as base text, I would justify that spelling not because it is the Arundel scribe's spelling — that's what Greg (1950–51) referred to as the tyranny of copy-text — but because it is the undocumented yet authentic Hocclevean form.

(Of course, in the very few cases where no clear analogy is provided by the holograph evidence, we have no alternative to accepting the form of the word provided by the *Regiment* scribe.)

Thus, and here I am merely exemplifying the results of applying the method set forth by Greetham, it is quite possible largely to construct Hocclevean usage and apply it to the text of the *Regiment*. But this still leaves unanswered the question of why one might want to do so, other than the problematic appeal of wishing to return via authorial forms to authorial intention. Rather than rehearsing familiar arguments against that possibility, it is more to the point to indicate why the holographs can't offer that kind of evidence. Most important of all, the holographs date from up to ten years after the completion of the poem, and so about ten years after the writing of the two earliest scribal copies. If we had a Hoccleve holograph of the *Regiment* from the time of the poem's completion, it would not be identical in its forms to a copy of the poem he could have written out a decade later, the time of the surviving holographs. Habits of writing change in time — an observation that has to be accepted by those who accept, as I do, that the Hengwrt and Ellesmere copies of the *Canterbury Tales* were the work of the same scribe.

In addition to the chronological gap between the *Regiment* and the extant holographs, there is a further gap between the Huntington and Durham holographs. In a recent essay, John Bowers (1989b) has written interestingly about the differences between Hoccleve's two holograph copies of *Learn to Die*, among other points calling attention to orthographic differences between the two manuscripts and the implications of those differences in authorial choice for textual theory and editorial practice. Thus, whatever else it is, the body of information stored in the holographs cannot claim to restore the orthography of the lost manuscript (whether presentation copy, or final draft handed to a better scribe for copying) that Hoccleve completed in 1411.

Why then might one want to turn to the somewhat anachronistic holographs in constructing a new edition of the poem? For a single reason: the holographs give access to a better text, a better poem, than one can obtain even from the excellent Arundel manuscript. For Hoccleve is not only a quite regular speller, he is also an extremely regular metrist — a point demonstrated at length in an important article by Judith Jefferson (1987). To cite but one telling statistic she provides: if you look at all the lines in the holographs which do not have an internal final 'e' and so do not raise the question of whether or not to pronounce final 'e' within the line, you find that 98% of those lines have ten syllables. This 98% statistic argues for a syllabic regularity even more notable than Hoccleve's fairly regular spelling practice. The implications of syllabic regularity for spelling were exemplified in my illustration of the two spellings of 'confort(e)lees' to fit two different metrical needs. What difference does this make when applying the holographs to the *Regiment*?

We can do no better than look at the first stanza of the poem, first as presented in Furnivall's EETS text, then in Seymour's *Selections*:

Mvsyng vpon the restles bisynesse
Which that this troubly world hath ay on honde,
That othir thyng than fruyt of byttirnesse
Ne yeldith nought, as I can vndirstonde,
At Chestre ynnë, right fast be the stronde,
As I lay in my bed vp-on a nyght,
Thought me bereft of sleep the [H:with] force and myght.

Musynge vpon the restlees bysynesse
Whyche that thys troubly world haþ ay on honde,
That oþer thyng than fruyt of bytirnesse
Ne ȝyldeth nouȝt as I can vnderstonde,
At Chestres Yn ryȝt fast by the Stronde
As I lay in my bedde vpon a nyȝt
Thogȝt me berefte of slepe the force and myȝt.

The stanza is apparently an unexceptionable example of decasyllabic verse — in fact, of iambic pentameter. For the fifth line, Furnivall reads: 'At Chestre ynnë, right fast be the stronde'. As noted earlier, the first leaf of Harley is missing, replaced by a modern hand copying from another manuscript.

It is of course Furnivall who puts the diacritic over the final 'e' of 'ynne', and the result is a regular, but also ungainly, iambic pentameter line. Seymour in his *Selections* records Arundel exactly: 'At Chestres Yn ryȝt fast by the Stronde'. This line thereby loses a syllable. Consultation of the sheet of variants for this line shows that the great majority of manuscripts give the spelling 'fast'. However, in the holographs Hoccleve uses that adverb 28 times, in every case spelling it with a final 'e'. Elimination of occurrences either end-of-line or elided leaves 7 instances, and in all of these pronunciation of the final 'e' is plainly called for: 'I am ny goon / as faste passe y shal'[3] or 'And to brynge it aboute he faste wroghte'[4] and so on. Chaucer too evidently always spells the adverb 'faste' and requires pronunciation of the final 'e' in the same situations: 'That highte the Tabard, faste by the Belle',[5] or 'This Nicholas his dore faste shette'.[6]

---

[3] *Learn to Die* (Durham, University Library MS Cosin V.iii.9), ed. Furnivall (1970, 203, l. 668).

[4] *Jereslaus' Wife* (Durham MS), ed. Furnivall (1970, 142, l.75).

[5] *Canterbury Tales* ed. Benson (1988, 35): GP, l. 719.

[6] *Canterbury Tales* ed. Benson (1988, 72): MilT, l. 3499.

In addition to this evidence in support of the reading 'faste', we can set the small fact that the five times Hoccleve uses the noun 'inn', it is spelt 'in' just like the common preposition, never 'inne' or 'ynne'. And so, with considerable and tedious labour over the two words 'inn' and 'faste', we have pretty certainly recovered authorial practice, and in so doing have made a better sounding line, contributing to a better first stanza. As with his later *Complaint*, Hoccleve's major poems begin strongly. In the structure of the first stanza, the iambic first line, with its first-foot inversion, initiating a main clause, is followed by a distinctly subordinate clause in the second line, which in turn is followed by two lines of in effect parenthetical subordination. It is only with the fifth line that the opening clause is developed, in what is a return from digressive subordination to the main issue, the speaker's here-and-now. This return to the main clause calls for, and in Hoccleve's spelling receives, the feeling of return conveyed by a completely regular iambic pentameter line. This line in turn leads, via the subordinate clause of the sixth line, to the powerfully condensed last line, with its first-foot inversion echoing that of the first line. Though Hoccleve is not always a careful poet, especially given his old reputation, it is important to pay attention to small matters which make all the difference between poetic skill and incompetence. This demonstration accurately reflects the nature of the contribution the holographs typically make — not big moves, but ones which give a better sense of what Hoccleve wrote.

As another example, Seymour gives this text for lines 1884–86:

'An egal change, my sone, ys in soothe
No charge. I wot yt wel inow, in dede.
What, sone myn, good hert take vnto the'.

That last line could be cited as a typical instance of Hoccleve's rigid adherence to mindless ten-syllable regularity,

with a distinctly awkward effect, until we discover in the
holographs that Hoccleve consistently spells the word for
'heart' *herte*, all 142 times, and that the three occurrences
without final 'e' signify 'hart, deer'. And when 'herte' doesn't
elide with a following vowel, it is always disyllabic: 'If thyn
hy herte, bolnynge in errour'[7] or 'For thanne in herte kowde
I nat be glad'.[8] So we rewrite line 1886: 'What, sone myn,
good herte take vnto the', an eleven-syllable line with a
feminine rhyme, a familiar pattern in Chaucer, with 'vnto the'
nicely echoing 'in soothe'.

A final and on the face of it bizarre instance of
Seymour's adherence to the tyranny of copy text, in this case
with no metrical consequence, occurs in the stanza in which
Hoccleve complains to the Old Man that six marks a year is
insufficient for his sustenance:

'Sixe marc ʒeerly and no more than that
Fader, to me me thynkyth ys ful lyte,
Consideryng how that I am nouʒt
In housbondrye ilerned worth a myte.' (974–77)

'Nouʒt' is indeed the Arundel scribe's preferred spelling
of the adverb 'not' — though he also spells it 'not', 'noʒt',
'nat', 'naght', and (though in rhyme position only) 'noght'.
Thus 'nat' rhyming with 'that' was available to him and
clearly the form called for here: for Arundel along with all of
the scribes exhibits a general decorum in usually providing
visual confirmation of rhymes. Now while Arundel and Harley
offer a repertoire of spellings for 'not', Hoccleve in his
holographs is exceptionally consistent. By far the preferred
form is 'nat'. Hoccleve's two alternative spellings are 'noght'

[7] *Address to Sir John Oldcastle* (San Marino, CA, Huntington Library
MS HM 111), ed. Furnivall (1970, 10, l. 49).

[8] *La Male Regle* (Huntington MS HM 111), ed. Furnivall (1970, 29, l.
131).

(22 times) and 'naght' (16 times). However, these numbers are misleading, for of the 22 occurrences of 'noght', all but two are end-of-line rhymes. As for 'naght', 9 of the 16 occurrences are end of line. But it is indicative of the semantic purposefulness of Hoccleve's spelling practice that in all but two of the seven seemingly exceptional cases, the word is used as equivalent to the noun 'nought' rather than the adverb 'not'. Thus: 'Thy cheer is naght ne haast noon eloquence'[9] or 'Elles myn art is naght, withouten drede'.[10] The four or five times when 'naght' or 'noght' occur as adverbs are unremarkable instances of careless spelling, surely not a bad record against the 550 'correct' uses, and shouldn't seriously impugn our sense of Hoccleve as a remarkably regular speller.

This may strike you as an exceptionally trivial point, and it is, except that its consequences are not trivial. Of an editor's following Arundel's rhyming of 'that' with 'nouʒt', one can only ask, what sensible purpose is served in faithfully recording a scribe's infelicitous slip? If the poet one is editing so obviously provides a standard spelling for the word 'not' when it isn't in rhyming position, why would one hesitate to replicate the authorial form where it is also the one obviously called for? These are among the elementary questions this edition answers and acts upon. Following authorial spelling, as we have seen, in a number of cases effects the very form of the verse. Once we have decided to observe spellings that preserve (or reconstruct) authorial versification, it follows that we will also observe spellings that don't have that function. And that procedure pretty well defines the scope and limits of the 'recovering' of authorial orthography. There are other

[9] *Balade to the Duke of York* (Huntington MS HM 111), ed. Furnivall (1970, 50, l. 25).

[10] *Jonathas* (Durham MS), ed. Furnivall (1970, 238, l. 626). Emended from Furnivall's edition, which incorrectly reads 'dreede' for MS 'drede'.

questions the edition must address, and at the time of writing not all of them have been satisfactorily answered. In particular, the earlier argument about the limited value of historical collation for establishing this text still leaves questions about the possibility of providing selective documentation for the relatively few instances of notable substantive variation, or the best form for presenting such information. Given the central importance of the use of holographs, it would be desirable to have a complete glossary, showing clearly which forms were reconstructions, or (in rare cases) scribal, and which documented holograph forms, but the economics of the edition might not allow for that luxury.

Returning to the use of authorial forms, it seems to me at once impractical and (except from an antiquarian viewpoint) pointless to try to preserve every feature of Hocclevean practice — the frequent use of 'þ' combined with raised 't' as an abbreviation for 'that', 'ff' for capital 'F', abbreviations for 'and', and the like. I am quite frankly selecting and defining that part of holograph practice which I judge to be significant for a modern reader interested in Hoccleve's language and verse. This will not satisfy those who believe that every element of recoverable practice is of potential significance and so should be preserved. But these features — including the not insignificant practice of pointing — can be adequately described and illustrated in the introduction, which will also of course include sections locating the work in its context as fifteenth-century poem, political document, and response to Lancastrian ideology and practice. In being thus selective in my use of holographs, I am implicitly calling attention to the fact that the edition is an act of reconstruction.

The distinguished text scholar and theorist G. Thomas Tanselle is one of those who very likely would not approve of the degree of departure from holograph data that I am here recommending. Yet in his brilliant little book, *A Rationale of Textual Criticism*, he provides a fine statement of just what I am attempting. He writes: 'Whatever concept of authorship one subscribes to, the act of reading or listening to receive a message from the past entails the effort to discover, through the text (or texts) one is presented with, the work that lies behind' (1989, 18). If the goal is 'the work that lies behind', then its recovery is necessarily going to be a work of reconstruction and interpretation, and what we construct and interpret can never be precisely equivalent to what left the author's hand or what is preserved for us in any surviving manuscript. It is worth recalling that the Hoccleve holographs were of little value before H.C. Schulz wrote his superb interpretation of them (1937). It is to be hoped that the new edition of the *Regiment of Princes*, drawing in part on those holographs, will assist the recovery, through reconstruction and interpretation, of Hoccleve's most famous poem.

Chaucer, Christine de Pizan, and Hoccleve: *The Letter of Cupid*

Roger Ellis

THIS paper needs to begin with a word of explanation, if not of apology. It started life at the Hoccleve conference as a paper on three of Hoccleve's minor translations: of the lyric on the Passion of Christ from Guillaume de Deguileville's *Pèlerinage de l'âme*;[1] of the chapter on the art of dying from Suso's *Horologium Sapientiae* included in Hoccleve's framed narrative collection, the *Series* (ed. Furnivall 1970, 178–212); and of the *Epistre au Dieu d'Amours* by Christine de Pizan, hereafter *Epistre*, a translation entitled 'Epistola [*var.* Littera] Cupidinis', hereafter 'Epistola'.[2] It sought both to identify

---

[1] For an edition of the Hoccleve lyric, see Furnivall (1970, 1–8); for a fuller version, Furnivall (1897, xxxvii–xlv); for comment, Seymour (1981, xiv n. 12, 103).

[2] For editions of the *Epistre*, see Roy (1891, 1–27) or Fenster and Erler (1990, 35–75): the latter is used for quotation in the present work, although printed from a different manuscript that wants four of the lines of the copy in Roy. There are two editions of the 'Epistola' in Furnivall (1970, 72–91, 294–308): the latter is from a Hoccleve holograph, now San Marino, CA, Huntington Library MS HM 744, where its title is 'Epistola'. Fenster and

Hoccleve's distinctive translational strategies in these works and, more ambitiously, to claim for him as translator the same playful way with words as is revealed in a number of his minor poems, for example the *Balade to Henry Somer* (ed. Furnivall 1970, 59–60). In addition, since two of the three original texts under consideration, the Deguileville and Christine de Pizan poems, were themselves extremely witty productions, I wanted to explore the extent to which Hoccleve's translations succeeded in preserving the wit of their originals, or generating something comparable, given, as Field (1989) and Beer (1991) have noted, that tone is one of the most difficult aspects of a work to translate. The exercise was inevitably partial; no study of Hoccleve as a translator would be complete that did not refer to his *Regiment of Princes*, or to the two translations from the *Gesta Romanorum* included as elements in the *Series*. Nevertheless, given that recent studies of both works by Hasler (1990) and Simpson (1991; 1995) have identified in Hoccleve's major works authorial strategies involving an active engagement with contradiction and opposition, within structures displaying a high degree of parallelism — in the words of Anna Torti (1991, 90), 'a play of reflected images, of analogies and dissimilarities' — it seemed worthwhile to make the attempt. In the event, the exercise had to be slimmed down yet further, to a study of Hoccleve's translation of the *Epistre*. The 'Epistola' has been studied as frequently as any of Hoccleve's

Erler also use this MS for their edition of the 'Epistola' (1990, 176-203) which is used for quotation in this essay. I give quotations from the *Epistre* by line number alone; those from the 'Epistola' are by line number preceded by 'l(l).' Translations from the *Epistre* are my own; Fenster and Erler also provide a translation, and see also Blamires (1992, 278–86) for a translation by Karen Pratt of extracts from the *Epistre*.

minor poems.[3] Nevertheless, we do not seem to have reached critical consensus on its achievement; so there may be some justification for starting a study of Hoccleve's translations with it. The question about Hoccleve's version of the *Epistre* — as easy to put as it is hard to answer — can reduce to this: how well does it capture the wit of its original? In the absence of a translator's prologue to provide a frame for the discussion, the only way to proceed is to identify, as far as possible, ways in which Hoccleve retains, and even reinforces, the elements of his original, and ways in which he simplifies or suppresses them.

I

Christine's *Epistre*, written in 1399, walks a tightrope, and the strain of its main project, the translating of antifeminist into profeminist tropes, frequently shows: but it also exposes the antifeminist assumption as *ex post facto* rationalizing. It has a number of ways of doing this. The most obvious is to counter commonplaces about fickleness in women, and about the noble men of antiquity whom they deceived (Adam, David, Samson, Solomon, 267–70), with commonplaces about virtuous women (168–78) and noble men who held women in proper regard (223–44) and were wronged, just like women, by other men (238). This involves the setting up of two kinds of writing in opposition, the one represented in the *Epistre* by Ovid and Jean de Meun (281–94, 321-22, 365–78, 389–96), the other — though Christine does not name any of the writers she depends on for it — by such as Albertano of Brescia in

---

[3] See in particular Mitchell (1968, 77–84), Fleming (1971), Bornstein (1981-82), Quinn (1986-87), Fenster and Erler (1990, 160–67); and brief comment in Pearsall (1977, 215–16).

the books he wrote for his sons as birthday presents.[4] But this replacement of one unreal extreme by another does not advance the argument very far. No more does the resolution of the 'debate', between Cupid and the embedded male voices he is answering, by appeal to higher authority, in this case the image of the Virgin Mary (571–88), in much the same way as happens in the Middle English *The Thrush and the Nightingale* (ed. Blamires [1992, 224–28]).

Slightly more complex is Cupid's use of the conventions of debate to reinterpret the offered evidence. While accepting the criticisms of the antifeminist tradition, he denies their blanket application to all women, and claims that only those who go against their nature deserve the condemnation (185–92, where the terms used anticipate those used later by clerics to attack all women, 379–81). He also reinterprets the figures used by the antifeminist lobby to prove its case (267-68, 319), in much the same way as Proserpine had done in the *Merchant's Tale* (2276–2302);[5] retitles Ovid's *Art of Love* the 'Livre d'Art de grant decevance … et de faulce apparence' [book of the art of great deception … and of false appearances] (377–78); and opposes the unfeigned 'semblant' of the female disciples of Christ (567) to the, frequently false, 'semblans' of male lovers (50, 53, 58, 134, 139, 526).

But there are more complex ways of deconstructing the antifeminist assumption. In the first place, the poem is so structured that a first section, concerning the active deceit of women by men and the boastful lies men tell one another about the conquests they never made, is followed by a second in which clerics, who either never had it, or are no longer up

---

[4] For a detailed account of medieval pro- and anti-feminist literature, see Blamires (1992); and, for brief comment specifically on Albertano's works, Benson (1988, 884, 923), and Blamires (1992, 237–42).

[5] In this paper, Chaucer's works are quoted from Benson (1988).

to it, traduce women by means of classical exempla, accusing women of the very vices — lying, for example (273) — of which they are themselves guilty (436). Literature and life thus connect in a striking inability of men to speak or write straight: accusation provides both pub rowdy and bookish scholar with a way of covering their tracks, as the repeated rhyme 'accuser ... excuser' (145–46, 275–76; cf. 137) implies. They also connect in the punishments which writers may bring upon themselves for their lies about women when they fall in love with women who precisely conform to and confirm the stereotypes of their imaginations. The 'vrayes histoires ancïennes/ De la Bible, qui ne peut mençonge estre' [true stories of the Bible, which cannot be a lie] (600–1), can thus be used to counter male lies (280), especially the lie that women tell lies (273). Besides, those same books which portray women so unflatteringly also show men in a bad light when they record the wars in which the latter have engaged (541–44).

As strong as these patterns of contrast, of course, are the patterns of likeness that link the two sexes, by means of which Christine is able still more subtly to deconstruct the antifeminist position. These include the repetition of a limited number of phrases and figures, applied now to women by the men who write about them, now to men by Cupid: verbal echoes which demonstrate that the two sexes are not simple opposites of each other. In this connection, two Biblical images are particularly noteworthy. One, of the tree and its fruit (751, cf. Matt. 12:33), reads the fruit as male and the tree as female so as to argue for male identification with, and dependence on, the female principle (every man had a mother, 169). The other similarly twists a Biblical commonplace, the creation of Eve from one of Adam's ribs, to imply that the temporal primacy of the male does not imply a corresponding material superiority: considered purely in terms of material origin, the female principle is as superior to the male as its material cause (Adam's rib) is more worthy than the material cause of man (the mud from which God formed him, 594–99). Given, moreover, a tendency of medieval thought to equate the female principle with matter and the male principle with form, it may not be completely accidental that Christine regularly describes God not as creating but as forming woman (591, 594, 603, 693), and once speaks of her as sharing the 'forme' of the Virgin Mary (581).[6]

This identification of men and women is reinforced by a number of other verbal details. 'Se desnature', for instance, is applied not only to women who act against their nature (678) but also to men who act against theirs in criticising women (181). The 'engin soubtil', by means of which the 'tres loyalë' Medea helped 'faulx Jason' win the Golden Fleece (437–39) — a rewriting of the story as found in sources like Boccaccio's *De Claris Mulieribus* and in the mythographic traditions[7] — echoes ironically the 'engin' and 'grant soubtiveté' needed to accomplish the seduction of the Rose in the *Roman* (401), as well as the sack of Troy, which functions as macrocosm to the former's microcosm (538, 541),[8] and characterizes clerics like Ovid who have written about both (306, 340, 387-88).

These same patterns are at work even in the smallest units of the sense. Female subjects of verbs are sometimes placed after verbs, and female objects placed before verbs, where the former can be read as direct objects of an implied male subject and the latter can be read as subjects of an action

---

[6] By contrast, God both 'fist et forma' the angels (193). For the opposition 'matter-form', see Blamires (1992), index *svv*; and, for recent comment on similar material in Christine's other works, Richards (1995). See also n. 14 below.

[7] Cf Heinrichs (1990), Blamires (1992), indices *sv*. Medea.

[8] On love and war as metaphors for each other in Christine, cf. 384–86.

involving an implied male object;[9] possessives and pronouns can be read as referring either to men or to women.[10] Admittedly, such features may not be peculiar to Christine's writing, but may generally characterize courtly French writing at the time (see further note 33 below); nevertheless, the uncertainties of interpretation to which they briefly give rise (who, that is, is doing what to whom?) prevent a simple or single reading of the text and may reveal all such readings as a form of *parti pris*.

But this obliteration of difference has the disconcerting effect of undermining the very ground on which Christine must take her stand: of deconstructing not only her opponents' arguments but also her own. The strain shows particularly in the way she has to accept the male terms of reference — that women are weak, for example — in order to construct her defence.[11] She is right to argue that, if woman is as weak as men claim, it takes the lover an unaccountable amount of time and effort to seduce her, and so too with the writer's telling of the story, in the *Roman de la Rose*. But, while the counterclaim that women are too weak to engage in the violent acts that men commit (warfare, for example, 641–48) argues for an innocence in women that men have lost, it may also imply that women are fatally easily deceived. Christine has to have it both ways, even as the male writers she is

---

[9] E.g. 's'aucunes attrayent en tel guise' (535), where Fenster and Erler translate 'aucunes' as subject of the verb ('and if some women act deceitfully'); since the line echoes 527, 'aucunes' should probably be read as direct object ('and if they [men] deceive some women in this way').

[10] E.g. 'et en courrous tost appaise son yre' (673), where Fenster and Erler translate 'when angry, quickly she allays her ire' (cf. Pratt [Blamires (1992, 285)]) but recognize that the phrase can also be read, as Hoccleve does, 'when her husband is angry she allays his ire'.

[11] This problem characterizes much writing by women in reaction to antifeminist writings: see, for example, Shepherd (1985).

challenging have done. Hence she has to work very hard to rescue Eve as symbol. It is easy enough to argue Eve's material superiority over Adam, as noted above: but such a view could easily shade into an assertion of moral as well as physical superiority, and hence imply Eve's greater moral responsibility for the Fall, a commonplace of antifeminist writing. So Christine, in arguing for Eve's innocence, very nearly turns her into a type of the gullible woman. To conceal the difficulty, she makes the meeting of Eve with the serpent a kind of antitype of the Annunciation ('et simplement de l'ennemi conceut/ La parole qu'il lui donna a croire', 608–9) [and simply conceived from the enemy the word he gave her to believe]. There is parallel if not precedent for this reading, for example in the wood block illustrations of the *Biblia Pauperum* (Henry 1987, 48); but the clear implication is usually that the antitype is more anti, so to say, than type. And elsewhere Christine has to admit that men and women were made of the same clay (749).

In much the same way, the presentation of the Virgin Mary as the archetype of womanhood leaves an unavoidable feeling, stronger in Hoccleve than in Christine, that difficult cases make hard law. In asserting the uniqueness of the Virgin Mary, Christine runs the risk of making her unavailable for purposes of comparison. In any case, she remains, in heaven as on earth, subordinate to the male principle of her son (583–84, 586–88). The antifeminist position may have been riddled with inconsistencies, but merely negating male objections point by point — accepting their inconsistent terms of reference to structure a defence — carries a danger of committing an equal and opposite error. Besides, many more men than the speaker is willing to name have a deservedly good reputation, even in France (245–58). If more good men exist than the poem is willing publicly to acknowledge, maybe more bad women do too: or maybe the whole thrust of the debate was misdirected.

These difficulties are brought into yet clearer focus by the speaker's ambiguous status as both male and divine. On the first point, Cupid's literary production shares with those of other male clerics the conviction of literature's exemplary and educational function: hence, like them, he teaches 'doctrine' (265–66, 764–67) by way of 'exemple' (246, 265, cf. below). But he must also differentiate his writings from theirs, which he does by asserting that, whereas they are all incurable liars (see above p. 32), he will have nothing to do with flattery and boasting (254–56, 755-56. On the second point, his religion stands in the same parodic relationship to Christianity as does the God of Love of the first part of the *Roman de la Rose* by Guillaume de Lorris: which makes the more ironic Christine's criticisms of de Meun's continuation of the work, since de Meun was merely making explicit the Ovidian frame within which de Lorris was covertly operating. As in the *Roman*, this parody religion comes with commandments (73), rewards for loyal service (769-70), and heresies to be shunned (691), and with a firm grasp of niceties of religious doctrine, like the importance of intention as an element in the commission of sin (615); the difference between mortal and venial sins (707–8); the obligation to hate the sin but not the sinner (only the sins should be publicly named);[12] and the distinction between the penalty attaching to a fault and the fault itself (*pena* and *culpa*, 689).[13] Yet this God of Love also shows, on occasion, a surprising lack of confidence in the power of his message to produce a good result in its male hearers,

---

[12] This is itself parodied when Cupid tells how he has refrained from naming the names of most of the men who served women honourably (254–56).

[13] Fenster and Erler's translation misses the point of this distinction, and renders it 'through suffering or pain' (cf. Pratt 'either torments or suffering' [Blamires (1992, 286)]). Christine's 'n'en peine ne en coulpe' (689) is a version of the tag 'a pena et culpa'.

preferring not to say all he knows for fear of incurring an angry response (625–37), and trusting that what he has said will not displease any male reader (665, 746). Even the female readers, who can be expected to identify with what he is saying, have to be encouraged to act upon it: the foolish, to model themselves on the good examples, and leave the bad (in the same way that the 'deffaillans' among the men were to take example from virtuous knights, 246); the good, to persevere in the course they have embarked upon (764–68). Authority deconstructs itself as tellingly here as does Chaucer's Nun's Priest.

These ambiguities were present in suspension in the *Roman*, but are much more clearly in evidence in a text which Christine may well have known, and which has to be taken into account when considering what Hoccleve made of her work, Chaucer's *Legend of Good Women*, where we have the same drive to rehabilitate virtuous women as animated the *Epistre*, and the same God of Love controlling the process. There are differences, of course. In particular, in the Prologue to the *Legend* Cupid both self-deconstructs and is deconstructed by the voices which answer his own, including a female voice notably absent from Christine's display of verbal cross-dressing. On the other hand, Chaucer's retelling of the stories of the virtuous women of antiquity, two of whom (Dido and Medea) also reappear, in summary form, in Christine, shares with the latter a need to suppress all evidence which might permit more usual, hostile, conclusions to be drawn about their characters. Thus, both Chaucer and Christine emphasize Medea's generosity in helping Jason to win the Golden Fleece, and Jason's unworthiness in abandoning her for another woman, but carefully omit all reference to her vengeful killing of the children she had borne him. In fact, allowing for the formal differences between the two works, Chaucer's presentation of his heroines in the *Legend* has to perform a balancing act not dissimilar to the one Christine's God of Love is engaged upon: though he gives the women little room for manoeuvre, Chaucer has to give them sufficient character to justify the feelings of sorrow he wants his narrative to generate. Similarly, though the male protagonists must be exposed as double-dealing, like most of Christine's male figures, they must display some vestiges of nobility so that the women can escape the charge of being too easily taken in by false appearance.[14]

Admittedly, we cannot be sure that Christine had read Chaucer. But other French writers contemporary with her had: Deschamps and the Duc de Berry, whom she knew personally; possibly Froissart; Oton de Granson.[15] In addition, she had connections with English nobility; her son Jean was in England from 1398, first as companion to the son of the Earl of Salisbury, then briefly, after 1400, under the protection of Henry IV.[16] To this indirect evidence of Christine's knowledge of Chaucer we may add evidence of other parallels

[14] Christine's inversion of the commonplace equation of male with form and female with matter (above p. 34) may also be paralleled in the *Legend* (1582–85).

[15] On Christine's links with Deschamps and the Duc de Berry, see Willard (1984, 45, 52, 56, 92, 100, 132, 187). On Chaucer's links with Deschamps, Froissart, the Duc de Berry and Oton de Granson, see Pearsall (1992, 68, 70–71, 130–31). Pearsall (1992, 130 n.3), thinks that Deschamps knew only of the translation of the *Roman* at the time of his poem in praise of Chaucer (for an edition, with translation, see Brewer [1978, 40–42]), though references there to Chaucer as an 'aigles' and to England as 'le regne d'Eneas' (ll. 5–6) might, in what Brewer calls an 'intensely artificial' work, provide a veiled reference to *The House of Fame*. Deschamps might also have known the *Prologue to the Wife of Bath's Tale* and the *Merchant's Tale*: see Thundy (1979) and comment in Ellis (1992, 134, n. 32).

[16] Campbell (1925, 658–60) gives the date of 1397 instead of 1398; for correction, deriving from Laidlaw (1982), see Willard (1984, 42–43 and n. 21).

between Christine's and Chaucer's works, notably, Cupid's declaration that the books which traduce women were all written by men — had women written the books, 'aultrement fust du fait' [the outcome would have been different] (418) — and, moreover, by old men no longer able to make love (493–504).[17] We can explain these parallels in one of two ways: either both writers drew independently on an, as yet, undiscovered source, or Christine was borrowing from Chaucer. Given the earlier-noted parallels with the *Legend*, the view that Christine was borrowing from Chaucer here strikes me as slightly easier to maintain: if so, she read Chaucer with a care to reproduce his ironies that she did not extend to her reading of Jean de Meun's continuation of the *Roman de la Rose*.

II

Hoccleve's version has two striking formal deviations from its original, regularly noted in earlier studies. (i) Only about half of the original appears in one form or another in the translation, and, at the same time, there are significant expansions to the text. (ii) Although the shape of the translation corresponds broadly to the shape of the original, at a few points Hoccleve translates material out of sequence. Of course, these changes may not have been intentional. On the first point, Hoccleve may have been translating from a copy in which the cuts and the additions first appeared; or he may have inadvertently omitted material from his copy by eye-skip. On the second, the scribe of Hoccleve's copy may have, deliberately or by accident, disturbed the order of his original, so that Hoccleve could not help but follow his source into error; alternatively, Hoccleve may have inadvertently disturbed

---

[17] For the Chaucerian parallels, see ProlWBT 688–710.

the ordering of the leaves of his own copy when working with it. Good precedent exists for the former practices in many translated works; as for the latter, we have an approximate parallel in the testimony of Caxton concerning the translation of the *Dictes and Sayengis* delivered to him by Earl Rivers.[18] Alternatively, the changes originate with Hoccleve's exercise of authorial prerogative. To decide the question one way or another is greatly complicated by the difficulty of determining exactly which parts of the *Epistre* Hoccleve has translated; from which copy of Christine's text;[19] and where in his poem he has translated them. Clearly, we need to be cautious in what we say about the translation: nevertheless, it seems to me very unlikely that we can explain the changes as the result of accident or inattention.

Thus, for example, ll. 148–224 of the 'Epistola' translate material from *Epistre* 185–298; these lines follow on from ll. 134–36, which had translated *Epistre* 165–67. If we except cuts to *Epistre* 200–60, and the creation of additional material ('Epistola' ll. 162–63 [cf. note 19 above], 179–89), the development of what we might call the narrative line of this

---

[18] For comment on Earl Rivers' translation, see Goodman (1991).

[19] The source of Hoccleve's translation lies in one of the group of manuscripts called L by Fenster and Erler, copies of an early version subsequently revised. Thus 'et supposé qu'il en y ait [L 1–3 qu'on en trouvast] de nices' (185) corresponds to 'al be it þat men fynde / o womman nyce'(l. 148); 'Je consens bien qu'elles n'ont pas les cuers/ Enclins a ce, ne a faiz de tel affaire' [L 1–3 ne a cruaute faire] (666–67), to 'wommannes herte/ to no creweltee/ Enclyned is' (ll. 344–45). The lines describing how one of the twelve apostles betrayed Christ (ll. 162–63) may have been inspired by lines about the apostles found in L 1–3 but missing in other manuscripts and in Fenster and Erler (after their line 560, Roy prints the following: 'Et meisement des Apostres les fais/ Qui pour la foi porterent maint dur fais').

passage fairly represents that of the *Epistre*. In the middle of this material, however, comes the following:

> O, euery man oghte han an herte tendre
> Vn to woman / and deeme hire honurable
> Whethir his shap be eithir thikke or sclendre
> Or he be badde or good / this is no fable
> Euery man woot / þat wit hath resonable
> Þat of a womman / he descendid is
> Than is it shame / speke of hire amis
>
> A wikkid tree / good fruyt may noon foorth brynge
> For swich the fruyt is / as þat is the tree. (ll. 169–77)

Line 169 derives probably from *Epistre* 168 ('car tout homme doit avoir le cuer tendre'), and thus returns us briefly to the section of the *Epistre* which was being translated immediately before the present one (as noted above, at 'Epistola' ll. 134–36). With line 173, however, we must look to *Epistre* 718 for a correspondence ('Je conclus que tous hommes raisonnables'), particularly since line 174 derives from *Epistre* 721 ('elles de qui tout homme est descendu'). Lastly, lines 176–77 come from *Epistre* 751 ('Car nul bon fruit de mal arbre ne vient'). Scribal inattention, by Hoccleve or in the copy from which he was translating, can hardly account for such a disturbance to the order of the *Epistre*.

Hoccleve, then, looks to have been acting not as scribe but rather as a *compilator* — if not as an *auctor* — in so rearranging the text of his original.[20] Occasionally these practices accompany, or produce, a subtle shift of meaning. Thus, when Christine positions the exemplary figure of the Virgin Mary before that of Eve, she seems to be wanting the reader to approach Eve through the grace-filled space that is the second Eve, so as to reclaim the first Eve from the attacks

---

[20] For these terms, see Minnis (1988, 94): source, St Bonaventura.

of the antifeminists. (Her presentation of Eve as mother, 605, is of a piece with her use of the mother-son metaphor elsewhere: cf. below p. 46.) Hoccleve places Eve before the Virgin Mary; slants her portrait so as to emphasize her disobedience (ll. 354, 378) and presumption (l. 355); and plays up the role of the Virgin correspondingly, so as to make her the positive of Eve's implied negative ('our lady / of lyf reparatrice', l. 403).

Nevertheless, Hoccleve's exercises of the compiler's function signify, in the main, only for the degree of familiarity with the details of the original which they suggest he must have had. In themselves they do not greatly signify, because the formal shape of the *Epistre*, elements of which have been noted above (p. 32), counts for less than what one might call its informal shape, the presentation and deconstruction of opposing points of view about women. Provided that the beginning and the ending were in their proper places so that the conventions of a letter were being properly flagged — and they are in place in the 'Epistola': cf. Fenster and Erler (1990, 167–68) — the translator had much the same licence to rearrange material in the body of his text as scribes had when copying out the tales of the 'great middle' of *The Canterbury Tales*; that same licence which the scribe of the Fairfax MS copy of Hoccleve's 'Epistola' gave himself when he reordered the text of the 'Epistola' more comprehensively than even Hoccleve had done the text of the *Epistre*.[21] And even then, the rearrangements sometimes have the effect merely of coalescing two different versions of the one commonplace. Similarly, and given the tendency of the *Epistre* to repeat itself, cuts to the text may not signify as greatly as additions to it, and will not be regularly considered in the following analysis.

---

[21] Noted by Fleming (1971, 22), following Furnivall (1892, 92).

By contrast with his cuts to the text, Hoccleve's additions
to it clearly signify: a consistent pattern of additions emerges
which shows him acting less as scribe and compiler, and more
as *commentator*.[22] In a translation the simplest patterns of
commentary occur, with great regularity, when the translator
provides explanatory glosses of his own for details of the text,
which elucidate obscurity and reinforce meaning. Those
probably occur in the 'Epistola': they certainly figure
prominently, as I hope to demonstrate, in Hoccleve's
translations of Deguileville and Suso. They are very likely to
occur in verse translations, even when the details being
translated are not particularly difficult: in such cases, as
Mitchell (1968, 76–77) has noted, the need to secure a rhyme
or fill out a line overrides other considerations. But the
translator could function as commentator in a more complex
way, interpreting the work he was translating through the lens
of another work, whose details he incorporated as appropriate
into the body of his translation alongside the original text.
Writers with literary aspirations seem to have used the practice
very regularly. Chaucer often reads one text through the lens
of another: Boccaccio's *Il Filostrato* by way of Boethius,
Trevet's story of Constance by way of Pope Innocent III's
De Miseria Humanae Condicionis, Petrarch's version of
Boccaccio's story of Griselda through the lens of an
anonymous French translation.[23] It is unsurprising, therefore,
that Chaucer's work, particularly the *Legend*, should provide

---

[22] The discussion in this paragraph means something different in its use
of the term *commentator* to what St Bonaventura meant (see further n. 20
above).

[23] This use of texts to interpret or mediate other texts almost comes to
be a defining feature of what Nolan (1992) has called the 'roman antique'.

for Hoccleve a gloss on the *Epistre*:[24] even as it may, in the *Epistre*, have acted as a gloss on the antifeminist tradition Christine was challenging. As is well known, Hoccleve refers to the *Legend* at l. 316 in the context of translated material on Medea and Dido; he also reworks its address to Dido (*Legend* 1254) into an apostrophe to the 'feithful womman ful of Innocence' who is deceived by false appearances (l. 41, cf. l. 91). But there is a difference between his use of the *Legend* and Christine's. If she cited Chaucer, Christine used him to undermine the antifeminist camp. Hoccleve uses Chaucer to reinforce a simplified version of Christine's party line, and to generate complications unrelated and even opposed to hers.

The process of simplification can be seen most easily in the central issue of male-female relationships. Christine's Cupid had allowed for virtue in men, and had acknowledged that men might be more virtuous than he was giving them credit for. In particular, he had come up with two figures especially worthy of commendation, Hutin de Vermeille and Oton de Granson (225–44). Hoccleve, who moved the action of the poem from France to England (l. 16) and the date of composition from 1399 (795–96) to 1402 (l. 476), could therefore have provided ready equivalents for these figures for his English readers, as he would later do in the *Dialogue* with his account of the Duke of Gloucester.[25] He does not do so:[26] moreover, he offers a straightforward condemnation of

---

[24] Chaucer's shadow falls similarly, if to a lesser extent, over Hoccleve's translation of the Deguileville poem.

[25] For the *Dialogue* see Furnivall (1970, 130-35), especially ll. 554–616, 631–37, 703–14.

[26] See Bornstein (1981-82) for a similar account of the reasons for their suppression; Mitchell (1968, 81) thinks their suppression a consequence of an English public's unfamiliarity with them (but see above n. 15 on de Granson, named in Chaucer's *Complaint of Venus*).

male duplicity which owes more to Chaucer's presentation of
the male protagonists of the *Legend* than it does to the
Epistre; which suppresses all Christine's qualified praise of
virtuous men; and which adds material of its own to blacken
them still more thoroughly (notably, a number of speeches
much livelier than anything Christine produced for her male
figures). Thus, though Hoccleve retains Christine's Biblical
metaphor of the tree and its fruit to explain the intimate
relations of the sexes (ll. 176–77), he returns the image on two
other occasions, for which the *Epistre* provided no direct
authority, to its more traditional religious and moral context,
so as to insist on the duplicity of men: men are a bad soil in
which 'trouthe' will never grow (l. 321), and they are 'croppe
and roote of gyle' (l. 17).[27] Just such a reading of the Biblical
image also occurs in the *Legend* (1368, 2395).

In much the same way, the women operate within a
simpler frame of reference than in the *Epistre*. One of the
distinctive features of the *Epistre*, from the very outset, was its
universalizing of the situation. Though the work tacitly
addressed noblewomen, it found all women, married and
single, noble and bourgeoise alike (11–12, cf. 404), implicated
in the unjust accusations men made against them. Likewise,
although a debauchee might well seek the company of
worthless women (330–35, 507–12), these are not directly
identified by class. The principal metaphor for the relation of
the sexes to each other is not one of class, but rather of
family: man should be to woman as a son is to his mother
(169, 729, 754). Hoccleve uses this metaphor once, but
changes it dramatically. Christine had written 'aux meres bien
ressemblent les fieulx' [sons resemble their mothers] (754); for
this Hoccleve gives us:

---

[27] The same metaphor is used to describe the women's complaint as a
'seed' (l. 11).

Take heede / of whom thow took thy begynnynge
Lat thy modir be mirour vn to thee
Honure hire / if thow wilt honurid be. (ll. 178–80)

As with his rewriting of the metaphor of the tree and its fruit, which immediately precedes the comment under consideration in both texts, Hoccleve insists upon reading Christine's words through a moral lens, in this case that of the Ten Commandments (Exod. 20:12), so as to imply that men need reminding of their duties, and that women exist to remind men of what they lack morally. Christine's idea of sons resembling their mothers as the fruit resembles the tree becomes, in the 'Epistola', a metaphor, common in Hoccleve's other works but not found in the *Epistre*, of an image seen in a mirror:[28] a metaphor too familiar nowadays from the pages of theorists to require comment. Indeed, Hoccleve's translation preserves the sense of a domestic context, so important as an element of Christine's thinking, only negatively: hence his added cynical comment, put into the mouth of an unsuccessful lover, that no man can fail if he have time enough, unless 'on maddyng he be so deepe broght / Þat he shende al / with open hoomlynesse', since women don't like that sort of thing (ll. 131–33); hence too the 'old prouerbe seid … in englissh' which warns men not to foul their own nests (ll. 183–89).

In much the same way, Hoccleve dilutes the force of Christine's arguments by making class a significant element of the poem. Where Christine, as we saw, represented all women as complaining at the wrongs done them, Hoccleve allows only the gently born a voice ('ladyes of honur and reuerence / And othir gentil wommen', ll. 9–10). These are set in a frame which Hoccleve received from the *Heroides* through

---

[28] For comment on this metaphor in Hoccleve see Torti (1991) and Simpson (1991).

Chaucer's *Legend*: acting in accordance with their courtly status, they are moved by 'pitee' (l. 43), set their false lovers in 'the weye / Of blisful loue' (ll. 47–48), and are promptly abandoned and publicly shamed by them. They are not permitted any other ground for their actions than 'pitee' (l. 72). Yet, even though they have given their bodies to be shamed by their lovers (l. 68), and might expect to share with them the 'ful greet repreef' due to both for their actions (l. 70), they are not allowed even that ground of their own to stand upon: they deserve not blame but thanks because they can help to meet men's needs (ll. 76–77).[29] Christine, by contrast, in a passage that Hoccleve does not translate, allows them more room for manoeuvre: they have the power to give men joy ('la riens … qui plus fait a tout homme de joye', 726–27: compare the men in Hoccleve, who are given 'ioie and teene' by Cupid himself, l. 242). Almost inevitably, in Hoccleve the women who deceive men are explicitly — as they were not in the *Epistre* — lower class figures:

> They [women] wiste / how sotilly / they [the men] kowde assaille
> Hem / and what falshode in herte they mente
> And tho Clerkes/ they in hir daunger hente …
> This ladyes / ne gentils nathelees
> Weren nat they / þat wroghten in this wyse
> But swich filthes þat wern vertulees. (ll. 255–57, 260–62)

Once the men have had their way with the mistress, it seems, they only have eyes for the barmaid (ll. 50–55): but these know better than the upper-class ladies what the men are up to, and beat the men at their own game. Interestingly, Hoccleve deconstructs his own deconstruction of Christine at this point, since these lower-class girls are credited with the

---

[29] For a different reading of these lines, which finds in them ironies akin to those of MerT, see Bornstein (1981-82, 8).

same quality to entrap their suitors as courtly romance regularly assigns to nobly-born women: 'daunger'. The picture is not an encouraging one, though: the greater the freedom of manoeuvre, the greater the wickedness, the lower the class.

Another added comment has the effect of identifying Hoccleve's voice, even briefly, with the male speakers in the 'Epistola'. Clerics have been sounding off, says Cupid, about the wickedness of women in the 'wikkid bookes' they write about them (l. 197). If, as seems likely, this detail recalls the book of 'wikked wyves' which the Wife of Bath's fifth husband read for pleasure (ProlWBT 685), it shows Hoccleve operating, like Christine, to undermine the antifeminist camp: not the subject-matter of the books is wicked but the intent of the authors. Later in the work, though, when the clerics are still sounding off about 'wommannes crabbid wikkidnesse' (l. 324), the speaker suddenly changes tack, with an apostrophe to the women:

> O, / womman / how shalt thow thy self cheuyce
> Syn men of thee / so mochil harm witnesse
> Yee / strah / do foorth / take noon heuynesse
> Keepe thyn owne / what men clappe or crake
> And some of hem shuln smerte / I vndirtake. (ll. 325–29)

The passage has no equivalent in the *Epistre*, nor in the *Legend*, though, as already noted, the latter was used in the 'Epistola' for passages of direct address to women (above p. 45). Its closest affinities are with the self-deconstructing *envoy* at the end of the *Clerk's Tale*, another work which praises women for their constancy in the face of male deceit and for their passive acceptance of the arbitrary exercise of male power. Here, undermining his own earlier identification of (lower-class) women and (immoral) action, Hoccleve allows all women the same power he formerly granted only to those of lower class, working in precisely the opposite direction to Christine, who read all women, so to say, from the top down.

Admittedly, the men don't have things all their own way. Unexpectedly, and by contrast with Christine's presentation of them, Hoccleve's narrative generates something approaching sympathy for them. In this context we may note the force of a repeated rhyme 'refuse ... muse', taken from *Epistre* 149–50. When first used (ll. 123–24), this rhyme speaks of the lady's refusal to accede to the suitor's 'musings', which provokes a cynical outburst against her (see above, p. 47); when used the second time, it speaks of the hapless suitor, for all his 'musings', being forced to accept 'the foulest slutte/ in al a town' (237–38). To complete the process of his humiliation, he is punished for his 'wrong ymaginacioun' against women (l. 235) — a quality he shares with Jean de Meun (l. 284), rather as Christine's Ovid shared with false lovers their 'soubtiveté' (above, p. 34) — by being driven to desire the favours of the town slut 'as thogh shee were a duchesse or a qweene' (l. 240). Given, as we have seen, that Hoccleve's poem is much more class-conscious than Christine's — the men go after the ladies first — the picture of the frantic lover conjuring Helen's beauty out of a brow of Egypt is as sad as it is funny. It also, paradoxically, reinforces the sense that, in love and out of love, men are victimized by their own imaginations, even as they respond to this victimization by making victims of women. (Christine, unsurprisingly, does not consider the way men's imaginations can trigger their relationships.) As another sign of sympathetic engagement with the male perspective, observe how the false lover, once he has abandoned his noble mistress, hastens to find and confide in his friend: till he can do so, 'his herte is on a lowe' (l. 61), as it would be if he were in love (ll. 239, 241). The model for this figure of the male confidant, who reappears later in the 'Epistola' (ll. 92–99), is not Christine but probably Chaucer (in his *Troilus*).[30] Christine has her man swapping playful stories not with a single friend but with numbers of companions in semi-public gatherings (taverns and courts: even the king's chambers, 108 ff). Her uncomplicated view of the homosocial bonding of dukes and lords, and, presumably, of the bonding between women as they come at the outset of the poem to appeal for justice, like the widows at the start of the *Knight's Tale*, simply does not allow for the loneliness of desire, nor for the pressure to confess, that the 'Epistola' fleetingly articulates.

In Hoccleve, then, the sexes are fairly rigidly confined within pre-determined roles, and isolated. What unites them turns out to be very different from the 'soutiveté' with which Christine was willing to credit them: quite simply, it is sin, from which 'vnnethes any' are free, men as well as women (ll. 379–97). Adam and Eve provide our basic role models, and they are in a 'semblable' case (l. 390) only because of sin: contrast Christine's use of the word 'semblable' to describe the relationship between men and women (731) and their cardinal role models, Mary and Christ (583). One gets the feeling that Christine is slightly embarrassed by questions of sin, and unwilling to find bad faith in anyone except the 'ennemi' of humankind (609). In the same way, since she wants to keep Mary as available as possible as an emblem of womankind, she tacitly identifies Mary with her divine election *by the mere fact of her creation*. Hoccleve, by contrast, makes Mary's election almost conditional on her superhuman absence of vice and fullness of virtue (ll. 404–5), which he describes in terms borrowed from the prologue to the *Prioress's Tale* (ll. 407–13, cf. PrT 460, 481–82). In this extremely orthodox reformulation of the *Epistre*, men are

---

[30] Other echoes of *Troilus* probably include ll. 17 (Tr II.348, V.1245), 24 (Tr III.1148, V.1435), 99 (Tr II.328, V.777).

utterly dependent on Mary's mercy: should that fail, 'farwel the ioie of man' (l. 415, a phrase which recalls the earlier-noted power of Cupid to bring 'ioie & teene'). Consequently, we should honour the Virgin 'and othir wommen alle / for hir sake' (l. 419).

Hoccleve thus, finally, endorses what Fleming (1971, 21) called Christine's 'essay in anti-antifeminism', but at the price of reinstating the very courtly positions, now applied to the Virgin Mary, which both Christine and her translator had understood to be another form of male fiction designed to deny the idealized female a voice and the capacity for action. Consequently, Christine's irony, which Hoccleve's translation has more or less preserved up to this point, disappears; so too does the sense of woman as a physical object (Christine's word for it was 'riens') with powers and desires of her own. Hence Hoccleve's ending, which idealizes women for their constancy (l. 447) and virtue (ll. 455–57, 461) by way of the exemplary virgin martyr St Margaret (ll. 421–27; her constancy is noted ll. 424, 433). But this puzzling choice of virgin martyr carries a final sting in the tail.[31] St Margaret, possibly a rewriting of a reference in the *Epistre* to St Nicholas (704), provides the occasion for obvious humour as Cupid has hastily to deconstruct the offered example: not her virginity but her constancy makes her exemplary, since 'ay We werreie ageyn chastitee' (l. 431). But this back-pedalling has the effect of detaching virginity from woman's exemplary function (seen most notably in the case of the Virgin Mary, l. 398) so as to expose the 'Epistola', like the *Epistre*, for the exercises in funambulism that they both are. However constructed, and regardless of who does the constructing, the

[31] For another explanation of the figure of St Margaret, see Fenster and Erler (1990, 163).

ideal woman turns out to be as slippery a shape-changer as the antifeminist lobby made her actual incarnation out to be.

A few observations are worth making, in conclusion, about the style of the translation. It approximates closely to Hoccleve's style generally. In particular, it reveals a preference for inversions of normal word order (patterns of auxiliary and infinitive; verb and direct object; especially auxiliary and past participle) in excess of what we find in the poetry of his contemporaries, even allowing for the need to distort word order in order to secure rhyme — where Hoccleve makes much use of the pattern infinitive-auxiliary — and in places where a normal word order would have been perfectly possible.[32] Hoccleve probably owes this style, at least in the 'Epistola', to Christine, who regularly practises it.[33] Other features of Hoccleve's versification already noted, like repeated rhymes and phrases, may also represent a response to the *Epistre*.[34] Unlike the uses Christine makes of such rhymes and of syntactic distortions to deconstruct the antifeminist position, though, I think these elements function

---

[32] E.g. 'spoken been' (l. 22), 'the man the pot hath' (l. 50), 'be waar sholde' (l. 212), 'felle can' (l. 234), 'him kepte' (l. 308).

[33] A particularly arresting example is 'quand decevoir l'omme et tempter la vient' (354) [when a man comes to deceive and tempt her]. Whether all such instances of Christine's practice should be read as a personal affectation or as a simple reflex of courtly French style I cannot be sure, though since Bruins (1925, 111–16) has distinguished Christine's practice from that of her contemporary Deschamps in respect of her readiness to follow the word order past participle-auxiliary, and from that of Froissart in respect of her readiness to follow the word order subject-noun object-verb, it may be that these, and other features noted earlier, actually characterize Christine's style. For argument in support of Christine's influence on fifteenth-century English prose, see Bornstein (1977), and comment in Ellis (1986, 116, n. 23).

[34] See Fenster and Erler (1990, 171) for comment on other possible debts of Hoccleve's versification and language to Christine.

more simply in the 'Epistola', as markers of the elevated, courtly style to which Hoccleve is aspiring.[35] Hoccleve's vocabulary is similarly elevated with words lifted direct from the French and not generally explained, including some, like 'entalentid' (l. 338, cf. 'entalenté', 566) which had only just appeared in English.[36] Alongside them, of course, we have the much more vigorous, and memorable, colloquialisms uttered by male speakers in the 'Epistola'. The two kinds of speech can neatly sum up Hoccleve's unbalanced, but distinct, achievement in the work.

[35] Cf. remarks on style in Chaucer's *Melibee* by Ellis (1986, 109–10).

[36] MED *sv*. The only previous example, in Chaucer, translates Latin 'afficiant'.

Hoccleve and ... Feminism?
Negotiating Meaning in
The Regiment of Princes

Catherine Batt

THE greater part of Hoccleve's *Regiment of Princes* is ostensibly a straightforward enough digest of received wisdom on the governance of kings, written for Prince Henry, possibly in 1411.[1] Yet the poem performs a curious balancing-act between an explicit and rigorous conservatism — as evidenced, for example, in its declared attitude to Lollardy — and something rather more individualistic, even wayward, in tone. The background to the *Regiment* proper is a long Prologue (constituting over two thousand lines of a text which runs to a total of 5439 lines), in which the Hoccleve character,

---

[1] References to the poem, by line number and in the text, are to Furnivall's edition (1897). The poem must have been written after the burning of the Lollard John Badby as a heretic, 5 March 1410, for Hoccleve refers to this event in the poem (286) and before 20 March 1413, when Henry IV died, for in line 816 he is 'þe kyng'. For a narrowing-down of the date to 1411, on the basis of further internal evidence and documentation of the delayed payment of Hoccleve's annuity, see Burrow (1994, 18) and Pearsall (1994, 387–88).

a government clerk beset by financial troubles and, sleepless with anxiety, himself in need of good advice, meets with an Old Man outside the confines of London. Conversation with the Old Man leads to the suggestion Hoccleve write his way out of his hardship with the production of a book of good counsel:

> '... þi pennë take, and write
> As þou canst, and þi sorowe tourne schal
> Into gladnesse ...'. (1874–76)

The Hoccleve persona's technique for establishing his credentials as advice-giver to Prince Henry has drawn a range of comment, from the view of Hoccleve as essentially a conservative (Pearsall 1994) to more sophisticated interpretations analysing the complexity of the relations between subject and king (Hasler 1990) and the means by which the writer finds his voice, both in literary and in historical terms (Simpson 1995).

 This paper attempts to define and account for the *timbre* of a brief passage towards the end of the *Regiment*, which declares itself a defence of womankind and her right to 'maistry' (5090–194), and to suggest how some attention to this part of the text might help identify a further perspective on Hoccleve's working-through of the relationship between writing, literary tradition and the historical moment. The *Regiment* proper is a work the contents of which the author has culled from various established pieces of advice literature, chief among them, he tells Prince Henry, Aegidius Romanus' *De Regimine Principum*, Pseudo-Aristotle's *Secreta Secretorum*, and Jacobus de Cessolis' *De Ludo Scacchorum* (2038–135). Hoccleve is selective of his sources, taking information from 'here & there' (2113) or 'plotmel' (2053), as he needs it. He divides his text into fifteen sections, dealing consecutively with the dignity of the monarch, the coronation oath, justice, the due observance of law, piety, mercy, patience, chastity, magnanimity, the unreliability of riches, generosity, avarice, prudence, good counsel and peace.

Hoccleve places his seeming defence of women in this final section of the *Regiment of Princes*, concerning peace and its attainment, and his argument turns upside-down the conventional biological determinism such as Aristotle offers and upon which the Church Fathers elaborate, which proclaims woman an imperfect adjunct to the male.[2] We learn how: 'sum nysë men, of lewdënesse' (5120), cite the crookedness of Adam's rib from which woman originates as evidence of her naturally 'crokid ... curtaisie' (5123). In response to this charge, Hoccleve argues that 'crokydnesse' tends towards the circular form, and since 'Cercly shap is most perfite figúre', geometrically signifying 'onhede', unity (5127–28), everything perfect must be circular:

> By-gynnë first at heuen, & rounde it is;
> Þe sonne and mone, & þe sterrës also;
> Hed of man, þen mouth, & hert, I-wisse,
> Ben allë rounde; and othir ben þer moo
> Than I expresse as now; but or I goo,
> 3it shal I bet wommannës part sustene;
> So biddeth pees, & þat to folwe I mene. (5139–45)

The difficulty these lines initially present is that of determining their register. Do they constitute a witty and playful reversal of a common set of assumptions, a reversal which none the less carries a serious feminist message (albeit one limited to the terms set up by women's detractors)? Or do

---

[2] Prudence Allen (1985) and Marie-Thérèse d'Alverny (1977) offer overviews of this material. Elizabeth A. Clark (1982) examines the ambivalences of John Chrysostom and Jerome's writings on women in the light of their friendships with women religious.

they, rather, border on the offensive?[3] How are we to understand the juxtaposition of those round parts of the male anatomy associated with the intellect, the affective, and their articulation, with — as I take it we are supposed to understand it — women's orifices? (Though this is an open issue in more ways than one, as the occlusion might signal male as well as female parts.) Is this suggesting a revolutionary placing of female sexuality, that is, in positive relation to the intellectual, or is it a conjunction pointing only to the ludicrous?[4]

In their ambivalence, the verses resemble other passages in the Hoccleve *corpus* seemingly addressing the status and nature of women, texts such as the *Epistola Cupidinis*, or *Letter of Cupid* (some of the rhetorical challenges of which Roger Ellis addresses in his contribution to this volume), and the famous references to its supposed reception by women that surface in Hoccleve's *Series*. In the *Dialogue* of the *Series*, the Friend who, tellingly enough, has not himself read the *Epistola*, assures Hoccleve that women have been offended by it, in spite of the author's protests that his poem 'concludith for hem / is no nay' (ed. Furnivall 1970, 1. 779).[5] The

[3] For Jerome Mitchell (1968, 29), Hoccleve here displays 'marked feminist sympathies'. On the other hand, Günter Hagel (1984, 182–88), can only read these same lines ironically. Examination of marginal notes in those MSS of the *Regiment* in the British Library (one of which, MS Royal 17.D.vi, bears the arms of Joan Neville, Countess of Salisbury), has yielded no clues as to contemporary response to these lines, whether from male or female readers. For a note on Joan Neville's association with the Royal MS, see Carol Meale (1993, 135).

[4] For an excellent discussion of how the sexual might be made relevant to the epistemological, in the context of the genre of fabliau, see E. Jane Burns (1993).

[5] The spirited discussion of modern critical debate over the author's intentions that prefaces the most recent edition of Hoccleve's *Letter of Cupid* (eds Fenster and Erler) concludes that Hoccleve is never so 'slippery'

Friend's recommendation is that Hoccleve should write something by way of a penitential exercise to expiate his offence to them, and the result is the tale of *Jereslaus' Wife*. Any good work this conservative text could possibly constitute appears undone when the Friend asks that Hoccleve write a tale warning his errant son against lecherous and avaricious women, to which request the author responds with the tale of *Jonathas* which, together with its prose moralization, concludes the text. In the *Series*, the issue of women's reception of literature, or perhaps more exactly, a man's construction, from a position of some ignorance, of literature and of women's responses to it, serves both to structure the collection as a whole, that is, itself to generate more writing, and to intensify the debate surrounding the disparateness and subjectivity of attitudes to literature in general.[6]

As far as concerns the *Regiment*, the delineating and delimiting of a female element, whether figurative or literal, serves a slightly different, but no less self-conscious purpose, for Hoccleve here shows himself highly aware of gender as 'a primary way of signifying relationships of power' (Scott 1989,

as on the subject of his attitude towards women (1990, 167). As Roger Ellis' contribution to this volume makes clear, the interpretative problem the *Letter of Cupid* poses is integral to its literary value. Anna Torti, meanwhile, resolves the difficulty of distinguishing between pro- and anti-feminist moves by constructing a Hoccleve who appreciates social dynamism while still in thrall to a conservative rhetoric: 'Some antifeminist overtones were inevitable, but the general impression is that by Hoccleve's time women had begun to play an active role in everyday life and that he could not avoid paying tribute to the status women had won for themselves' (1992, 273). This 'solution', however, bypasses rather than analyses Hoccleve's self-conscious manipulation of rhetoric.

[6] For different perspectives on the literary and political implications of naming a woman, 'my lady of Westmerland', as the final dedicatee of the *Series* (ed. Furnivall 1970, p. 242), see Winstead (1993) and David Mills' contribution to this volume.

95). Through examining this issue, in the main part of the *Regiment* and its Prologue, as well as in the intriguing immediate context of the lines quoted above from the passage on 'maistry', I hope to uncover something about the nature and purposes of Hoccleve's irony, and his conception of how the literary relates to the political, in the context of his understanding of and his relation to contemporary political affairs.

Although I've just claimed a central position for gender in the *Regiment*, it is the organizing frame gender provides, rather than any pressing need for its analysis, that seems important, in the prologue at least. For those binary oppositions conventionally predicated on sexual difference — intellect versus body, power versus disenfranchisement, centrality versus marginality — are part of the discourse the Hoccleve figure uses, and ultimately transcends, in describing his own predicament. As he articulates his position, so he imagines himself in those very spaces traditionally understood as 'feminine'. One might assign to Hoccleve here the state of 'feminization' that Elaine Tuttle Hansen points out in an analysis of Chaucer and his works, and which she defines as:

> … a dramatized state of social, psychological, and discursive crisis wherein men occupy positions and/or perform functions already occupied and performed, within a given text and its contexts, by women or normatively assigned by orthodox discourses to Woman. (1992, 16)[7]

---

[7] H. Marshall Leicester's remarks on the relation of masculine to feminine in the *Canterbury Tales* in general are apt here too:

> There are no masculine or feminine subjects in the *Canterbury Tales*; there are only "masculine" and "feminine" positions with which subjects have to deal and in relation to which they have to place themselves. (1990, 217)

Yet this placing also needs some qualification, for in the prologue to the *Regiment*, the emphasis is not only on the adoption of a quasi-feminine role, but also on what I should term a 'colonization' of 'feminine' space. Because the material and the symbolic elide in the history Hoccleve offers of himself and his environment, on the figurative level there occurs a complementary 'masculinization' (albeit limited) of what medieval writings often conceptualize as feminine. This makes for a greater fluidity in the rhetorical means available for representation, especially the representation of the self, but also has a dislocating effect on the possibilities for the representation of 'real' women, the issue of their political status, and a consideration of their symbolic importance, which in turn has implications for how we understand Hoccleve's broader literary and political project, particularly towards the end of his poem.

In the lengthy Prologue to the *Regiment*, Hoccleve portrays himself at a depressive *impasse* which the good offices of the Old Man he fortuitously meets serve to unblock, for this figure, as we have seen, recommends he write a book of advice for Prince Henry as the surest means to relieving his poverty. In the course of this *mise-en-scène*, as in the *Regiment* proper, Hoccleve offers us a deft critique of advice literature and the power bases on which it rests, the interdependence of poet and patron and the precarious nature of the writer's position and that of the hierarchical structure he appears to defend, as recent studies point out (Hasler 1990; Scanlon 1990; Scanlon 1994). And Hoccleve appropriates the terms of those traditionally politically disenfranchised. Even as he writes himself into the role of advice-giver, he displays those qualities antifeminist literature especially condemns in women: he wanders aimlessly about, he is prey to excess, as is his poem (Hasler 1990, 177–78), and he is overly garrulous. This last trait he marks out to his interlocutor as a fault, in a register that both belongs to the penitential (for it echoes Chaucer's Parson's warning against 'jangling' and 'clapping'), and declares a social impropriety for which it is women who are usually chastised:

> 'I am right sikir it hath ben an helle,
> Yow for to herken me þus iangle & clappe,
> So lewdly in my termës I me wrappe.' (1034–36)[8]

These lines introduce a recurrent theme in the dialogue, a strong appeal to the Old Man, 'My fadir dere' (1041), to take on a confessor's role, and the language of social and spiritual elide in Hoccleve's petitioning for both the latter's 'grace' and his good advice (1041–43). As Hoccleve gradually writes himself from margin to centre, the articulation of a 'public' language of literary allegiance merges with, and then overtakes, the 'personal' discourse of the confessional. Hoccleve draws attention to this transition by claiming the influence of another 'father', Chaucer (Hasler 1990, 174 and n. 29):

> 'O, maister deere, and fadir reuerent!
> Mi maister Chaucer, flour of eloquence,
> Mirour of fructuous entendëment,
> O, vniuersel fadir in science!' (1961–64)

As we will see, however, the explicit and apparently straightforward invocations of paternity and orthodoxy do not account fully for the nature of the literary and social

---

[8] For an accessible representative sample of antifeminist literature and the terms in which women are castigated, see Blamires (1992). Hoccleve here appropriates the vocabulary of the *Parson's Tale* where the preacher admonishes: 'Janglynge is whan a man speketh to muche biforn folk, and clappeth as a mille, and taketh no keep what he seith.' (ParsT l. 405, in ed. Benson [1988]). All future references to *CT* are to this edition, by line number, in the text. The envoy to the *Clerk's Tale* exhorts wives: 'Ay clappeth as a mille, I yow consaille.' (ClT 1200)

continuities Hoccleve establishes in this poem. The
'colonization' of a 'feminine' space, while it enlarges the area
of self-definition for the Hoccleve persona, also offers, I will
argue, another, transgressive, means of conceptualizing both
authorial strategy and the function of the written. In the
Prologue, however, Hoccleve as persona appropriates feminine
spaces while also concretizing abstract concepts as masculine
in such a way as to articulate a relationship between the
symbolic and the literal which relates specifically to a
masculine political self-definition.

The narrator's chance meeting with the Old Man
constitutes of course the Prologue's highly pragmatic rewriting
of Boethius' *Consolation of Philosophy*, one in which
philosophical consolation takes second place to recognizing
the necessity of material well-being. The stranger interprets
himself as an *exemplum*, one who in Age regrets the follies of
Youth, and in what we might call his 'historically specific
role' in his dialogue with the Hoccleve figure, he highlights
the social reciprocity essential to advice literature. The Old
Man takes on Lady Philosophy's role, but his comfort lies less
in resignation than in helping to redefine in highly pragmatic
terms the meaning of poverty for individuals. Correlative to
this masculine replacement of an authoritative female
personification in a discussion about practical necessity and
political action is the tendency to present as male those
embodied concepts that answer most nearly to Hoccleve's own
condition: thus Sleeplessness, 'Wach' (76), and the
'encombrous' (185) Anxiety that weighs him down, 'þoght,
my crewel fo' (73), are masculine, while Rest, whom Anxiety
has chased away (73–74) is feminine, as is Stability:

> Than deemed I that seurëte would nought
> With me abyde, it is nought to hir pay,

Ther to soiurne as sche descendë may. (38–40)[9]

The conceptualization of 'present' political and immanent qualities as masculine here produces an ambivalent effect: it gives a semblance of cohesion to the disparately and subjectively-constituted masculine 'person' of Hoccleve, defined against a set of elements which, because absent, are imagined as 'other'. At the same time, because such conditions as Rest and Stability are both desirable and necessary, Hoccleve's person cannot be integral without the assimilation of these other elements, as yet absent, and imagined as feminine.

The *Regiment* proper does not maintain this tendency to characterize as female those concepts or material conditions that appear conspicuous by their absence or their alienation, perhaps because the latter part of the text focuses more on the conventional means of constituting the monarch than on defining a language to describe the present condition of the advice-giver. Thus the sections of advice to Prince Henry offer female personifications of both the positive and the negative, including Law, Justice and Generosity, but also Avarice, who 'may … vndo a kyng / Thurgh hire insaciable gredynesse' (4481–82). In the Prologue, however, on the figurative level,

---

[9] The impulse here is perhaps similar to that behind Guillaume de Lorris' portrayal of *Bial Acoil*, 'Fair Welcome', in the *Roman de la Rose*: as the aspect of the Lady most compliant with the Dreamer's wishes, he is also male; and *Dangier*, 'Resistance', or 'Rebuff', who displays a typically masculine aggression and violence, is a monstrous male (tr. Horgan 1994, 43–44). Colette Murphy (1994) offers an analogous explanation for the sex of Lady Church in *Piers Plowman*: in this text, the disjunction between herself as female and other, and the Dreamer as male, limits her usefulness to him as a spiritual guide: see especially pp. 146–48, and p. 157: 'The Church, in its idealised abstract form, is engendered in a female body, but this is inadequate for the Dreamer: he needs to know in ways which relate to his experience.'

masculine and feminine are made intrinsically part of Hoccleve's self-definition, and his 'lack' imagined in feminized terms.[10]

How might such a shift in the terms of a figurative language relate to the presentation of 'real' women in this poem? Obviously, feminine personifications are by no means indicative of historical women's political power, but imagining the abstract as gendered is not incidental to the perception of social and political order, and other fifteenth-century authors also recognize the potential personification has to express the relationship between the literal and the figurative, especially in terms of affording space to, and defining, the feminine. In his *Troy Book*, for example, Lydgate makes a direct link between the changeableness of Fortune, 'Selde or nat feithful ouþer stable' (ed. Bergen 1910, Bk V, l. 3548), the inevitable fickleness of Criseid, and the natural instability of women in general, as Anna Torti (1989) has pointed out. Torti suggests also that we have here *in parvo* a microcosm of the vicissitudes of the war itself (1989, 180), though this reading would seem to require a somewhat gender-blind good will. Then again, this is perhaps the point: for we also have to consider the significance in the poem of the peculiar self-cancelling procedure Lydgate employs when he translates Guido's antifeminist asides on the Troy narrative and then excuses himself by saying that he is obliged to follow his

[10] It is perhaps significant that mention of Chaucer gives an extra fluidity to personification: in the Prologue, Hoccleve describes how a masculine Death has slain his master, but Chaucer's writings succeed in confounding Death (1965–74). In the Proem to the *Regiment* proper, Death is female, one who is indiscriminate in her treatment of eminent and ignoble alike, by whom 'euery man is maistried' (2098), and who has carried off Chaucer in spite of his fame.

source.[11] Lydgate appears at one and the same time to engage in an easy equation between historical women's nature and symbolic representation in general, while laying the status of antifeminist rhetoric open to question.

In the *Regiment*, meanwhile, Hoccleve's apppropriation of gendered personifications in order to construct his own nature scarcely overturns the whole system of representation.[12] For example, the sexualized portrayal of Fortune both Hoccleve (66–68) and the Old Man articulate in the Prologue is hardly radical. The latter tells how in old age he is unattractive to Fortune — 'straw for impotence! / Sche loueþ yong folk, & large of dyspence' (1392–93). But in this context, the link between the emblematic and the social is assumed rather than open to analysis, and reflects on the Old Man's perspective, not woman's nature. Where the *Troy Book* offers us Criseid as control, as a means to interpreting women's behaviour, here we have an absence, or at best a displacement, of women as subjects and agents. The Prologue makes little mention of women, apart from the Virgin Mary and Hoccleve's wife, whom it presents as, respectively, a facilitator and an obstacle. Invocation to the Virgin serves to emphasize Hoccleve's orthodoxy, while Mrs Hoccleve features indirectly to expose the ultimate inseparability of public and private as far as concerns her husband's political fortunes, rather than in her own right, or within an examination of

---

[11] In Book III of his *Troy Book* (ed. Bergen 1908, ll. 4344–45), Lydgate observes that Guido enjoys speaking 'cursidly' of women 'þuru-out al his bok': he himself then repeats his source's diatribes against women, together with apologies for so doing, accompanied by somewhat over-vigorous defences of womankind (see, for example, the 'reprefe' of women he reproduces in the section on Medea, in Book I [ed. Bergen 1908, ll. 2100ff.]).

[12] Hoccleve is also traditional, for example, in having the Old Man refer to the soul as 'wyf' to God (1349).

personal relations. Thus Hoccleve explains that marriage has debarred him from a career in the Church (1447–50). And while the account of Hoccleve's marriage, entered into 'Only for loue' (1561) has been read as an innovative and touching defence of 'modern emotionality' (Classen 1990, 173), the Old Man's prurient interest in his charge's sexual activities also mark them out (somewhat hilariously) as another area of human existence subject to private confession made public and to penitential regulation:

> 'Þow demest lust and loue conuertible,
> Per cas .../... art þou oght, sonë myn, sensible
> In whiche cas þat þou oghtest the for-bere,
> And in whiche nat? canst þou to þis answere?' (1563–68)

The Old Man goes on to fulminate against those exogamous matches in which the nobility engages for financial gain, and against the social disruption adultery engenders, with a wealth of examples drawn from what he claims is present English aristocratic practice, and from scripture (1667–764). In this light the emphasis on love, defining women in terms of private space and sexual function, serves as a move to depoliticize marriage and indirectly (because this appears to be their only mode of attaining influence) to depoliticize womankind.

The political arena, then, is masculine and accordingly the subjection to power as well as the exercise of power express themselves in the *Regiment* overwhelmingly with reference to men. Men's, rather than women's, bodies are subject to violence in *exempla* describing the workings of power. Thus an evil judge is flayed and his skin covers the judgement seat his son occupies, so as to encourage the latter in the exercise of justice (2675–88). A handsome youth disfigures himself in order to avoid women's sexual advances (3718–31). Yet Hoccleve omits anecdotes from his sources that define women as dangerous because actively sexual within the political domain. For example, in the section dealing with the desirability of chastity in a sovereign, he neglects a startling little fable, from the *Secreta Secretorum*, about sexual relations, in which 'Aristotle' reminds Alexander of how he prevented him from having anything to do with the woman bred up on poison by a vengeful Queen of India bent on his destruction: 'thy deth shold have come to the thurgh the ardure that thow sholdest have in flesshly delyng with her' (ed. Manzalaoui 1977, 46). The same part of the *Regiment* tells of how the daughters of a certain duchess place rotting chicken pieces under their armpits and breasts, the stench of which repulses their would-be rapists, leading the author to apostrophize:

> O wommanhode! in þe regneþ vertu
> So excellent, þat to feble is my witt
> To éxpresse it; wherefor I am eschu
> To melde or make a long sermoun of it.
> Som mannës mouth yit wolde I were I-schet,
> That vice of wommen spareþ nought bywreye,
> ffor allë soothës ben nought for to seie. (3788–94)

This sounds not unlike the 'pro and contra' method Lydgate employs, as we saw above. Had Prince Henry read Jacobus de Cessolis' *De Ludo Scacchorum*, as the poem suggests he had, he would have known that Hoccleve's *occultatio* refers to the narrative that frames what in this version is solely an account of successfully defended honour.[13] For it is the duchess herself who has put her daughters in danger by falling in love

---

[13] The only copy of Jacobus de Cessolis' work I have been able to trace to Henry's ownership is the one on the list McFarlane reproduces, of books acquired after the siege of Meaux in 1422 (1972, 233–38), but it seems more reasonable to accept that Henry would have known those books of advice, Jacobus' among them, that Hoccleve mentions as familiar to him (2129–35), than to take for granted the Prince's ignorance.

with King Catanus, to whom she offers the surrender of her
besieged fortress should he promise to marry her. The
description of the duchess's fate is not for the faint-hearted:

> And hit happend than that the kynge Catanus toke acordyng
> to his promyse the duchesse and lay wyth her one night for
> to saue his oth And on the morn he made her comune unto
> alle the hungres [his troops] / And the thirde day after he
> dyde doo put a staf of tre fro the nether part of her / thrugh
> her body unto her throte or mouthe / for because of the lust
> of her flessh she betrayed her cyte and sayd suche husbond /
> suche wyf &c.
>
> (*The Game and Playe of the Chesse (1474)*, ed. Axon
> 1883, 34–35)[14]

It seems typical of Hoccleve's ambivalence on the subject that
he should spare us such a deeply misogynistic treatment of
women's rule while at the same time signalling its omission.
Writing women out of the political equation does not serve to
address the issue of their involvement in public affairs.

Hoccleve, then, plays with and skews binary systems of
power relations, writing himself from margin to centre as he
takes on the role of advice-giver, and making his
garrulousness constitute the text. Through the alternating
evocation of exemplary models and an emphasis on the
historical moment, he also suggests that human experience is
ultimately containable neither by fixed precept nor by any one
particular register. But it seems that any analysis of women's
situations or their public roles falls casualty to his particular
method of exposing social constructions. With this in mind, I
want to return to consider more carefully the section of the

---

[14] I cite Caxton's translation here for convenience, as it follows the
Latin original closely at this point, and is in general more easily available
than the Latin text (for which, see Kopke 1879).

poem prefatory to the section on peace and to understand its workings in its immediate context.

The most obvious clue to our reception of the verses on women in the final section of the *Regiment* is the eulogy of Chaucer as 'firstë fyndere of our faire langáge' (4978), which bridges the section on good counsel and the initial description of peace. The portrait of Chaucer famously accompanying these lines testifies to the vernacular writer's importance and influence, and Larry Scanlon has recently commented on it as exemplary of how 'Hoccleve consistently locates Chaucer's authority biographically' (1994, 312). For Scanlon, the move from text to image acknowledges the extent to which the textual depends on 'the actualities of historical existence' (1994, 313): ultimately, Chaucerian authority cannot inhere in his texts alone, but is tied to his person, to the historical moment. Scanlon's emphasis on immediacy is valuable, as is his observation of the structural importance to Hoccleve of what he calls 'the trope of voice' (1994, 322): Scanlon makes such stresses part of a broader argument which links the moral and cultural authority of English vernacular literature with the Lancastrian regime's consolidation of its own power (an argument with which Fisher [1992] and Pearsall [1994] would agree).

I would argue, however, that one might read differently both what the portrait signals about the structuring of the poem, and the importance to advice literature of the relation between previously-encoded wisdom and the historical moment. With the graphic index of Chaucer's importance, Hoccleve assures us that he is presenting us in good faith with a portrait that will keep the master in our memories. This establishment of literary origins simultaneously works to assure the reader of the present author's religious orthodoxy: the emphasis on the visual as pious commemoration and as memory-aid aligns Hoccleve with those who condemn the Lollard resistance to images. At the same time, explicit mention of Chaucer alerts us to the political possibilities language has and to which the earlier author draws attention.

Furthermore, the manuscript executions of the Chaucer portrait themselves intimate different ways of interpreting the earlier poet's influence. In British Library, MS Harley 4866, fol. 88r, which Furnivall reproduces in his edition of the *Regiment* (1897, p.180), the Chaucer figure, extending an arm from the background frame that contains him, provides the index to the lines referring to him. The cruder figure that appears in BL MS Royal 17.D.vi, however, though his hand still indicates the line referring to 'peyntynge', sprawls across the page in rather less determinate relation to the words, in such a way as to signal a different kind of influence, one articulated in words in the lines on women's rule that follow.[15] Before the appearance of the portrait, Hoccleve has characterized Chaucer as a new Tullius (2085–86), his wisdom recuperable as general encoded precepts of wisdom on which the later poet depends, though he falls short of him in expression (4978–81). For Hoccleve, Chaucer's influence functions at both a local and a more general level: I would suggest that the 'defence' of women's sovereignty positioned after Chaucer's 'physical' appearance, like the Royal MS illustration, offers another, albeit oblique, commentary on the nature of Chaucer's influence on the whole poem, one which suggests a different perspective on the relationship between advice-giver and advice-receiver, author and patron, the written and its reception, and the relation between encoded wisdom and present political action.

[15] Derek Pearsall reproduces both pictures in Appendix A to his biography of Chaucer (1992, 285–305), the Harley MS on p. 286, the Royal MS on p. 290.

The section on Peace promises closure to a self-declaredly written text, one which calls on another written text as its authority:

> Touche I wol heere, of pees, a worde or two,
> As þat scripturës maken mencïoun,
> And þan my boke is endid al, and do. (5020–22)

But not only does the narrator emphasize the performative aspect of the words that follow, and the particularity of the voice that delivers them: the lines preface a sequence that demonstrates how the dynamic of the whole poem as advice literature requires completion by the book's recipient, Prince Henry. For this is the section in which Hoccleve finds his most forceful voice as adviser, where authoritative prescription meets contemporary political experience, and present events firmly relegate exemplary past narratives to a secondary role: 'to sekë stories olde / Non nede is' (5287–88). Lamenting the internal strife of England and France, he will both suggest a holy war as a means to unity, and recommend a marriage alliance between England and France as the means to cement peace:

> Purchaseth pees by wey of marïage,
> And ye þerinne schul fynden auauntage. (5403–4)

This reading of the contemporary scene was certainly not new; state documents reveal that moves for a royal marriage between the Prince of Wales and, as the text has it, 'aliqua de filiabus … de Francia' were being made in 1406 and although there is then a hiatus, the issue is taken up again in 1414. What is less certain is that it was in any way a priority in 1411–12, at the time Hoccleve is writing.[16] And while

---

[16] For the relevant documents, see the *Foedera*, ed. Rymer, Vol. 8 (1710, 435), and Vol. 9 (1712, 208–15). I wish to thank Professor Christopher Allmand of the University of Liverpool for his generous help

Hoccleve appears to be drawing on current affairs for his
suggestion for policy, he also explicitly cites the *Revelations*
of St Bridget of Sweden (5384–97), where Christ recommends
peace be effected between England and France by means of
marriage, and that their kings unite to defend Christendom, as
an endorsement of his advice to the Prince.[17] As Henry was
to found a Bridgettine monastery at Syon in 1415, the charter
of which declared its main function was to pray for peace, one
could view Hoccleve's argument as explicitly mirroring the
Prince's concerns. But Henry's devotion to St Bridget appears
to have been encouraged primarily by Henry Lord FitzHugh
(Allmand 1992, 274–76), and again, it is not exactly clear
whether Hoccleve, at the time he is composing the poem, is
recommending, anticipating or echoing what later emerge as
Henry's political and cultural interests and conscious policies.

So what is the status of the good advice Hoccleve offers,
counsel which refers to what might have been in political
terms a highly sensitive subject? The section troping women's
claims to sovereignty goes at least some way to answering this
question. As in the preceding part of the *Regiment*, there
seems here to be little correlation between historical women's
experiences and the terms in which their 'maistrie' is

on the question of marriage negotiations with France in the early fifteenth
century. Günter Hagel (1984) argues with reference to this topic that
Hoccleve is in no way a propagandist of the Crown's policies, but is
motivated primarily by a profound longing for peace.

[17] For Christ's words, see the *The 'Liber Celestis' of St Bridget of
Sweden* (ed. Ellis 1987, 344–45). Christ describes himself as 'verray pees'
(344) and while He threatens that those, on both the English and French
sides, who do not make peace will be punished, He reserves for the king of
France the need for humility, 'verray mekenes' (345). In an article on the
dissemination of St Bridget's work in England in the fifteenth century, Ellis
notes Bridget's support of the English, and mentions that excerpts from the
Revelations were used to bolster English claims against France (1982, 173).

discussed. Hoccleve's own neglect to expand on the future queen's role, and his references to widowhood (5219–22) and rape (5335–37) as central features of contemporary unrest, would seem to draw further attention to this disjunction. We might read the gap between language and experience as exposing a lack of political language for women, but for the fact that there *is* available a discourse (however anxious) about the power of the female sovereign, with which Hoccleve could have engaged had he so wished (Fradenburg 1992; Strohm 1992, 95–119). Hoccleve seems in general to have given little thought to women's political voice. As we saw above, he accepts the validity of St Bridget's *Revelations*: but in the *Address to Sir John Oldcastle*, he is unequivocally negative about women's involving themselves in disputation over issues which, he claims, they don't understand. The vehemence of his opposition is probably directed more against Lollardy, however, than against the principle of women aspiring to learning:

> Some wommen eeke, thogh hir wit be thynne,
> Wole argumentes make in holy writ!
> Lewde calates! sittith doun and spynne,
> And kakele of sumwhat elles, for your wit
> Is al to feeble to despute of it!
>
> (ed. Furnivall 1970, ll. 145–48)[18]

If we move from responses to specific examples of women's political involvement to the general question of the representation of women's power, however, we might say that the lines embedded in the Peace section certainly convey a sense of entrapment for women. The 'cercly shap' figuratively circumscribes our representation, setting the very subject apart

---

[18] For a discussion of the nature and extent of women's involvement with the Lollard movement, see Margaret Aston's chapter on 'Lollard Women Priests?' (Aston 1984, 49-70).

from other references to women in the rest of the poem. In Hoccleve's political philosophy, 'women' are largely an absence, something unsaid, even faintly 'obscene' in the sense that the space to which he has relegated them is beyond certain boundaries of representation. But it is precisely the gap between a factually-retrievable reality and literary representations of women that makes anti- and pro-feminist argument the most self-reflexive and opaque of literary debates, the most self-conscious, and the most in need of extratextual reference in order to fix its meaning. To invoke again the lines on 'roundness' and perfection (5139–45): the other 'round thing' indisputably present in the poem is the rotund figure of Chaucer himself, reference to whom, whether direct or oblique, highlights questions about how one formulates the potential for language's political value, specifically within the *Regiment*.

As the Peace section unfolds, Hoccleve moves from scriptural authority to the interrelation of the social and spiritual and the need for inner tranquility in the attainment of Peace: but he frames his 'pro-woman' argument with warnings against the perniciousness of 'false pees', such as that between Adam and Eve, where reason fell prey to sensuality, making for a 'haynous' accord which is inimical to 'goodë pees' (5095–96). Hoccleve's discourse is a literary patchwork. He anticipates — and in doing so constructs — women's censure:

> If þat þis come vnto the audience
> Of women, I am sure I shal be shent:
> ffor þat I touche of swich obedience,
> Many a browë shal on me be bent;
> Thei willë wayten been equipollent,
> And sumwhat morë, vnto hir housbondis,
> And sum men seyn swich vsage in þis lond is. (5104–10)

Yet his tone seems calculated less to appease his audience than to compound his offence, as he follows John Chrysostom

(Clark 1982, 5) in reading Eve's transgression as explanatory of modern women's disobedience. It is telling that, having written 'real' women out of the proceedings, Hoccleve writes them back in as the site of anxiety over reception (a technique he similarly employs in the *Series*, as we saw above, and in which, moreover, the Friend introduces that male creation, the Wife of Bath, as 'auctrice' that women are not pleased to have men accuse them of faults [*Dialogue*, ll. 694–97]). In the *Regiment*, Hoccleve then ironically closes down that reception with a *chleuasmos*: if women object, he implies, it is because they are precisely what he says they are.

Taking as a given the masculine premise, which the Wife of Bath endorses, that women want sovereignty, Hoccleve puts forward, in support of his argument, details he appears to have borrowed from Christine de Pizan's *Epistre au Dieu d'Amours* (eds Fenster and Erler 1990, 62, ll. 591–604), where, in promotion of woman's dignity, rather than of her absolute sovereignty, Christine has pointed out that Eve was made not of earth but from Adam's noble rib, that God formed her in Paradise and, furthermore, that He Himself honoured all womankind in being born of Mary (ll. 572–84).[19] Hoccleve recontextualizes and modifies these points, and supplements them with an observation, from Augustine, on Eve's typological value: she represents the institution of Holy

---

[19] It is interesting that Hoccleve does not retain these lines in his earlier English reworking of Christine's poem, the *Letter of Cupid*. Nor, in that adaptation, does Hoccleve seem particularly interested in woman's autonomous dignity. Where, for example, Christine emphasizes women's innate qualities of mildness, compassion, humility, piety and generosity (eds Fenster and Erler 1990, 66, ll. 668–80), Hoccleve stresses a positive but auxiliary role for women:

And wel they can a mannes ire asswage
With softe wordes discreet and benigne. (194, ll. 341–42)

Church and her sacraments (5160–66). That Woman should be
especially praised for Eve's usefulness as a metaphor alerts us
to the figural nature of the 'defence' of women in which this
comment is embedded.

Within a passage that emphasizes again and again the
sense of text as performance — 'a-gayn þat, strongly wil I
replie' (5124): 'ʒit shal I bet wommannës part sustene' (5144):
'ffor morë haue I for hir partye ʒit' (5160) — Hoccleve works
himself up to counter triumphantly the scriptural authority that
says women allowed free rein will be naturally contrarious:

> Þe text is such, I woot wel, but what þei?
> That text I vndir-stondë þus al-wey:
> Whan þat housbondës hem mys-take and erre,
> Ageyn þat vicë wyuës maken werre. (5184–87)

The lines, though they do not claim to *be* her voice, echo the
Wife of Bath in ideology — women want sovereignty — and
in ideolect (for example, in the tone of its engagement with
authorities: compare 'That gentil text can I wel understonde'
(ProlWBT 29). The passage's closing couplet offers a
chiasmus ironically reversing the original remarks on unruly
peace:

> Goode is [a husband] suffre; therby pees may spring;
> Housbondës pees is pesible suffryng. (5193–94)

This elegantly confirms and develops the opinion of the Wife
of Bath's reported animadversion to her husband on the
subject:

> 'Suffreth alwey, syn ye so wel kan preche;
> And but ye do, certein we shal yow teche
> That it is fair to have a wyf in pees.
> Oon of us two moste bowen, doutelees,
> And sith a man is moore resonable
> Than womman is, ye moste been suffrable.'
>
> (ProlWBT 437–42)

If Hoccleve in the Prologue conveys a sense of being less than 'complete' through the alienation from himself of a series of desirable conditions and qualities he personifies as female, here he would seem to reclaim an integral nature by means of an invocation of a female impersonation that complicatedly reclaims, and presages the completion of, his role as advice-giver and writer. This 'completion' of his function as writer of advice literature is of course achieved less through the apparent 'defence of women' than through the reference to Chaucer this rhetorical sleight-of-hand invokes. This has implications for both 'master' and 'pupil': Hoccleve's mimicry appears here to be reinvoking Chaucer to show how his influence manifests itself in unexpected and less orthodox ways than his portrait solemnly endorses. But there are other reasons for introducing this dissenting and uncontainable voice, reasons that reflect on advice literature itself, and to appreciate fully the ironies of this passage, we need to look beyond the Wife of Bath to Chaucer's most able female adviser, Prudence. In *Melibee*, Prudence also has to justify herself as an advice-giver by arguing against her husband's objection that: 'Jhesus Syrak seith that "if the wyf have maistrie, she is contrarious to hir housbonde"' (Mel 1059). Prudence denies this is a recommendation to ignore one's wife's voice completely, claiming instead that a wife must step in and prevent her husband from doing evil, countering bad advice with good:

> 'Thus sholde ye understonde the philosophre that seith, "In wikked conseil wommen venquisshen hir housbondes."'
>
> (Mel 1094)

I would argue that in the *Regiment* Hoccleve is condensing and refracting an important aspect of Chaucer's own formulation of how advice literature operates.

In *Melibee*, the prose Canterbury Tale privileged by virtue of being told by Chaucer the pilgrim, the male

protagonist comes to accept the advice of his wife to forgive
those who have wronged him, and thus gain the political and
moral advantage. *Melibee* works on both a broad political and
on a personal level, as a 'Mirror for Princes' and also as a
book about self-governance: Prudence is both a 'good wife'
and that aspect of a man's rational faculty that understands the
good sense in pragmatic counsel — in prudence, that is.[20]
But Prudence has to struggle against Melibee's resistance to
taking advice from a woman, and the site of that struggle is in
part an argument about how to constitute the authoritative
proverbial, and in what terms one is to interpret it. Chaucer-
as-Pilgrim already draws attention to the importance of the
proverbial in this narrative, in the lines that preface it:

> ... I telle somwhat moore
> Of proverbes than ye han herd bifoore
> Comprehended in this litel tretys heere,
> To enforce with th'effect of my mateere. (ProlMel 955–58)

The declared emphasis on proverbs seems more tactical than
descriptive of Chaucer's practice in translating Renaud de
Louens' *Livre de Melibée et de Dame Prudence*. As Larry
Scanlon has noted, *Melibee* poses generally the question of
how one is to translate written authority into action, and how
the written relates to the political (1994, 206–15).

But Chaucer, through the female authority figure who
initially provokes anti-feminist proverbs from her husband as

---

[20] Lee Patterson points out the significance of Chaucer's naming
Melibee's wounded daughter Sophie, 'Wisdom', and suggests that through
her Chaucer signals that true wisdom falls casualty to a pragmatic know-
how in 'a world of relentlessly prudential imperatives' (1989, 160).
However, Prudence's promise to Melibee that following her advice will
restore his daughter to him — '(I)f ye wol triste to my conseil, I shal
restoore yow youre doghter hool and sound.' (Mel 1110) — also intimates
the possibility that prudence and wisdom might not after all be mutually
exclusive.

arguments against her counsel, and who then reinterprets those arguments to her advantage, also concerns himself with the interpretation of the proverbial. The tale demonstrates the extent to which what is apparently 'common wisdom', the mainstay of advice literature, is itself open to debate, subject to a dynamic in which personal and social interests are continually in play. The fluid meaning of the apparently 'fixed' proverbial is shown most prominently in Prudence's situation and argument, while the disconcertingly broad possibilities for the interpretation of particular metaphors further stress the need for awareness of literary and social context to determine meaning. For example, Melibee, bowing to his wife's better judgement, tells her she exemplifies Solomon's observation:

> 'wordes that been spoken discreetly by ordinaunce been honycombes, for they yeven swetnesse to the soule and hoolsomnesse to the body.' (Mel 1113)

Melibee's ertswhile enemies tell Prudence they have been won over by her words, which prove Solomon's dictum that 'sweete wordes multiplien and encreescen freendes' (1740). Yet elsewhere, 'honey' words are dangerous: Prudence tells Melibee himself that his name means 'a man that drynketh hony', not because he has absorbed her counsel, but because he has fallen prey to the temptations of the world (1410–12) and to the sweet words of flatterers (1177). The double significance of Prudence herself — as 'outside influence' and as aspect of Melibee's psyche — further emphasizes the interaction of text and subject, the way in which meaning and political responsibility do not pre-exist as a 'given', but are negotiated by individuals in the very act of participating in language.[21]

Hoccleve has already implicitly acknowledged the influence of the *Melibee* on the *Regiment*, in the sections emphasizing the ruler's need to exercise prudence and counsel (4747–77), which echo some of the tenets of *Melibee* and declare Chaucer to have written 'in caas semblable' (4979) regarding the reception and uses of counsel. Where the portrait of Chaucer in the *Regiment* consolidates and celebrates a position for Chaucer as a good counsellor, the new Tullius (who replaces the Tullius whose authority Prudence asserts in *Melibee*, e.g., 1165), the following section on women and 'maistrie' acknowledges, if it does not precisely re-enact, Chaucer's method. Hoccleve's allusiveness demonstrates an awareness of how Prudence and the Wife of Bath offer different approaches to the question of the sententious and its capacity for both commentary on, and the constitution of, the subject and one's relation to the world. The pragmatically-constituted advice literature of *Melibee* recognizes the means by which the proverbial is open to interpretation, while the Wife of Bath's very construction interrogates the relation between the socially-enacted and the rhetorically-encoded. Chaucer would seem to address the political aspect of language through women's voices because the proverbial supplies a predetermined (and also contradictory) assessment of their nature which particularly concentrates those issues of responsibility and agency.

---

[21] For a different interpretation of *Melibee* which also reads Prudence metatextually, see Judith Ferster (1985). Ferster suggests that women characters in the *Canterbury Tales* figure generally the difficulties of textual hermeneutics, and that Prudence, because she cannot necessarily control how Melibee will interpret her words, is both 'a figure for the author and demonstrates the perils of narration.' (1985, 21)

The 'defence of women' section which 'speaks' Chaucer, with its lively awareness of the text as performance, and of the influence of audience reception, demonstrates that Chaucer's legacy is not a fixed encoding of the proverbial but rather a recognition of plurality contingent on the interaction of writer and receiver's culturally-perceived and determined stances. The final section of the *Regiment* suggests that for Hoccleve, such a recognition leaves the aware writer with a burden of responsibility, in that it urges political action and engagement (or at least its articulation), here in the form of practical advice on contemporary issues. Accordingly, Hoccleve makes recommendations for the future good of the whole state, and is at the same time anxious that the prince should safeguard his well-being as one of his subjects (Simpson 1995, 180).

Unpacking the influences upon Hoccleve's advice writing still leaves unresolved the problems of reception. What kinds of response might the form of the 'defence of women' signal or encourage or acknowledge? And what might its encoding reveal of the political climate in which it was written? The passage is open to several interpretations. We could see its quasi self-containment as indicative of a kind of literary exercise insulated from the real world, the principal value of which is as display. This might be a possibility were Hoccleve in a political position he perceived as potentially dangerous. So one might argue Prince Henry can read this, and by extension the whole poem, as a piece of rhetorical *léger de main* that doesn't ultimately directly implicate him (even though the text proposes a marriage alliance for him as part of a plan for peace). The contradictions in the text — for example, the Old Man's moral opposition to exogamy in the Prologue ('Weddyng at hoom in þis land, holsom were ...' [1674–80]), and the later recommendation that the Prince marry a French princess — might, if it were necessary, support the author's plea that the text was more playful than serious. The passage on women's 'maistrie' might then be seen to function as an implicit statement about censorship, of the kind Lev Loseff delineates in his account of 'Aesopian language' in Soviet literature (1984).[22] Such an interpretation would assume a negative view of Hoccleve's ability to influence policy, whether as government clerk or as poet, and would restrict appreciation of the implications of a rhetorical knowingness to the (one must then assume) politically disenfranchised literati, and preclude action. Alternatively, were one to follow the argument of such as Pearsall (1994), who sees Hoccleve as primarily in the pay of the Prince, Hoccleve's outrageous defence of 'crookidnesse', if taken uncritically within an antifeminist tradition, advertises and recommends its author as an able propagandist.

A final suggestion returns us to the evidence of Hoccleve's Chaucerian 'inheritance', and hangs on the nature and political influence of what I would loosely term a 'literary' court culture (though it is of course unhelpful to distinguish absolutely between 'literary' and 'political'). A reader of medieval literature cannot study the passage without being aware of its Chaucerian subtext, which alone appears to supply us with a coherent reading of all its elements. In recognizing a Chaucer-derived, obliquely-stated multiplicity of possible meanings, one accordingly and inevitably participates in a world of social engagement, exchange, and responsibility, of the kind we witness, albeit in a different and apparently more narrowly literary context, in those fifteenth-century collections of dream and debate poetry, in which originally separate works might comment on, challenge, and complement one another by virtue of their contiguity (Lerer 1993; Boffey 1994). Appreciation of such a culture would have been a part of Prince Henry's education, as far as we can reconstruct it

---

[22] I am grateful to Elizabeth Maslen of Queen Mary and Westfield College, University of London, for bringing this text to my attention.

(Orme 1989), and I would argue that literature's sophisticated interpretative strategies suggest a less rigidly-prescribed relation between vernacular writings and the king's exercise of political power than, for example, Scanlon (1994) would claim.

Lee Patterson has characterized Chaucer as:

> … the originator of a national literature in a culture that lacks both the concept of literature and a social identity for those who produce it. Lacking a recognizable role within the social whole, Chaucer is obliged to locate himself outside it.
>
> (1989, 135)

But there is space for a more optimistic reading of the Chaucerian influence Hoccleve inscribes in his poem, one that sees cultural and literary claims as not distinct from, nor subordinate to, but as exercising a more positive and sophisticated hold on the political than we might think possible in contemporary culture, an influence that would make the writing *and* the reading of the *Regiment* fully an act of reciprocal political engagement and responsibility within the terms of political awareness Chaucer's language promotes.

The Voices of Thomas Hoccleve

David Mills

Introduction

IN the 1980s and 90s Hoccleve has proved responsive to a variety of critical approaches. The earlier biographical fascination of the 'good harmless fellow, who has read with advantage many books'[1] projected by the *Series* has been promoted to the status of a psychological case study of mental breakdown, its diagnosis and medieval attitudes towards it. The historical Privy Seal Clerk has been reclaimed as a commentator within a wider concept of historical culture, highlighting the implicit relevance of the poetry to its contemporary political context.[2] And in the light of modern literary theory the *Series* has been revalued from a skilful utilization of literary genres (Thornley 1967), to a more boldly

[1] B. ten Brink (1893, 215). Hoccleve's reputation is perceptively discussed in Bernard O'Donoghue's introduction to *Thomas Hoccleve: Selected Poems* (1982).

[2] David Lawton (1987, 761–77). See also Scanlon (1994), Pearsall (1994).

innovative enterprise, the 'early transformation of the narrator
and the medium from a method of relating a fiction to the
very subject of that fiction' (Greetham 1988-89, 245), or a
self-reflexive form of writing 'whose single unifying plot is
the story of its own composition' and 'the story of a poet
negotiating a new relationship with his audience' (Simpson
1991, 20, 22).

At the heart of this exciting diversity of approach lies the
problem of reconciling the self-reflexive and the historical —
or, as others have rephrased the dichotomy, the private and the
public or the inner and the outer.[3] Hoccleve's poetry exists at
the interface between the two 'areas', however defined. He is
a social poet. He realizes poetry as a social activity, the
writer's entrance-currency into the social world, but because
its genres, themes and values are pre-determined by the
society to which it is addressed, the two-way communication
of writer and reader serves also as a metaphor for social
relationships. In the *Series* Hoccleve challenges conventional
notions of structure, sequence and social and literary values
and, by juxtaposing different registers, demonstrates that the
poet loses himself as he seeks to satisfy demands from his
readers that are contradictory and encounters interpretations
that are mistaken. Unconfidently seeking readmission to his
former social circles, the Narrator of the *Series* offers to
conform to both the literary and the social expectations of the
society that encloses him but remains pathetically at the edge
of that society.

---

[3] 'Inner and Outer' is the title of the chapter in which Stephen Medcalf
discusses Hoccleve (Medcalf 1981, 123–40).

Building a Poem

Part-way into the *Dialogue*, the Friend offers the Narrator some familiar advice about undertaking a commission for his patron, Duke Humphrey:

> 'Thow woost wel / who shal an hous edifie,
> Gooth nat ther-to withoute auisament,
> If he be wys, for with his mental ye
> ffirst is it seen / pourposid / cast & ment,
> How it shal wroght been / elles al is shent.' (638–42)[4]

Geoffrey of Vinsauf's well-known analogy in *Poetria Nova* between building in stone and in words stresses the need for prior planning, a mental shaping of the whole work to ensure a proportioned structure. The allusion to this injunction at this point in the work, however, serves to highlight the apparently haphazard structure of what E.P. Hammond revealingly termed the *Series* (1969, 69). It indicates that Hoccleve is aware of the normative expectations of poetic structure against which the *Series* responds. Characteristically, the allusion is not merely aesthetic. The Narrator is seeking an appropriate text to translate for his patron and planning is also a matter of social diplomacy and a decorum of subject and style for the reader: *avisament* is used here with both the reflective sense of 'consideration, reflection, forethought' (MED 2) and the social senses of 'advice, counsel' and 'consultation, conference' (MED 6 and 7).

This advice reminds us of the very different spirit in which the *Complaint* began. From the start Hoccleve plays upon the reader's generic expectations to achieve his effect. The Prologue to the *Complaint* suggests the conventional

---

[4] All quotations are from Furnivall (1970). References are by line number, in the text.

connection between the passing year and the passing life of Man:

> how welthye a man be / or well be-gone,
> endure it shall not / he shall it for-gon.
> deathe vnder fote / shall hym thrist adowne:
> that is every wites / conclusyon. (11–14)

where the final generalization (*every wites*) wittily encompasses the double sense of *conclusyon* as 'destiny, fate' and 'inference' (MED 2b and 3). From this unexceptionable generalization we seem to move predictably towards the Narrator's particular situation:

> … my wite
> to lyve / no lust hadd, ne [no] delyte. (27–28)

The poem announces itself as a conventional meditation upon the transitory nature of life, a generic expectation which is not — at least immediately — fulfilled.

Not only is the subject not achieved; the meditational tone which the poem's slow and measured opening stanzas create yield suddenly to a violent and impetuous conclusion:

> The grefe abowte / my harte so [sore] swal
> and bolned evar / to and to so sore,
> that nedes / oute I must[e] there-with-all;
> I thowght I nolde it kepe cloos no more,
> ne lett it in me / for to olde and hore;
> and for to preve / I cam of a woman,
> I brast oute on the morowe / and thus began. (29–35)

The energy of these lines takes the reader by surprise. The physical force of *swal and bolned*, the insistent rhythm of *to and to so sore*, and ellipsis of *nedes oute I muste* in the first three lines contrast with the reflective style of the preceding stanzas. *Grefe* here has physical impact. *I thowght* conveys an active intent, not detached reflection, which is strengthened in *I nolde*. The *Complaint* emerges here not as a considered and planned structure but as a violent outpouring of pent-up feeling. *I brast oute* not only suggests the immediate confrontation of poet and paper, but also the release of the individual from his own emotional prison. Writing becomes an escape from this emotional prison, further justified as a mark of the narrator's common humanity (*for to preve / I cam of a woman*). The *Complaint* is his response to his own inner anguish, which otherwise would be unnaturally suppressed.

This powerful stanza is not only tonally different from what has preceded. It takes up and inverts themes already introduced. *oute I muste* reverses *hervest Inned* (1); *swal and bolned* reverses *chaunge sank into myne herte roote* (7); the denial of *olde and hore* picks up *the broune season* (2) and *colowre of yelownesse* (5). Paradoxically, the season of death is, for the narrator, a time also of regeneration. The grief within him bursts out and impels him to write. Poetic rebirth springs from a time of decay, and the theme of death yields to the more immediate theme of change and social alienation. The poem's elegiac opening will not be followed through. Its 'complaint' is of grievance rather than lament, and its dissatisfaction combines with a recurrent strain of rejoicing at deliverance from illness which culminates in its final celebratory stanzas. We seem not to be in the pre-planned and controlled world of Geoffrey of Vinsauf. So successful is this pose that H.S. Bennett complains:

> He is an egoist, and the naive outpourings of his own hopes and fears are presented to us in all their crude immediacy What his mind thought his pen set down without much preliminary attempt to control or refine his matter in a clear picture. (1947, 149)

Bennett's comment indicates how convincingly Hoccleve has held together two meanings of *compleint* — its personal sense of 'lamentation' (MED 1(a)) and its generic sense of 'a plaintive poem, a plaint' (MED 3), a public document. The

Friend's concern draws attention to this semantic blurring. He seems initially shocked at the determinedly personal and subjective character of a work to be released into the public domain ('forthe to goo', *Dialogue* 23). The Narrator has invested a public genre with individual touches and proclaims its personal application in referring to it as 'my "complaynt"' (*Dialogue* 1), a possessive which he characteristically withholds from the other, translated, works that make up the *Series* ('this booke', *Joys of Heaven* 918; 'this tale', *Jereslaus' Wife: Epilogue* 2). The Friend resists this possession with its subjective implications, referring to the work merely as a written text (cf. 'this complaynte', 23) but finally accedes to the Narrator's usage ('thy compleynt', 200), partly (as we shall see) as a pacifying strategy to the then impassioned Narrator.[5]

Bennett's psychologically informed criticism of the historical Hoccleve is, however, misleading. The reader is repeatedly reminded that the *Complaint* is a shaped and considered piece of writing. The Prologue is not only an explanation of but also a justification for the *Complaint*, as if the *Complaint* cannot stand alone. The refusal to *it kepe cloos* is a refusal not only to sit brooding inwardly but also to conceal the grief from others. As we learn from the *Dialogue*, the poem is written not only for the expression of personal feelings but as a communication to a wider audience, and the *preve* of humanity is as much for his friends' information and their accusation as for his own relief. Self-expression and the need to communicate with a wider audience combine. Viewed as a social document, the self-justifying Prologue becomes an apology for the unconventional character of the poem, but that impression is created by allusion to the conventions from which it departs. As Simpson points out, both the rubric that

---

[5] I am grateful to Catherine Batt for pointing out this detail to me.

follows the Prologue and the reading of the *Complaint* to the
Friend insist upon its status as a written text (1991, 18). That
awareness also invites us to view it as a literary artefact,
completed and objectively appraised by writer (Narrator) and
reader (Friend). The opening line of the *Dialogue*, 'And,
endyd my "complaynt" / in this manere', foregrounds the final
stanzas of the *Complaint* as a self-conscious literary device of
closure within the conventional consolatory *topos*. By the end
of the *Complaint* the Narrator has constructed himself as an
exemplum of patience.

Alienation

Hoccleve's preoccupation with illness in his poems has
its roots, as Penelope Doob has shown, in the traditional view
of illness as the consequence of sin which must be confessed
in order that God and Mary, the healers, can cure the sufferer
(1974, 210–13). But in both *La Male Regle* and the *Series*
illness is important for its enduring social consequences rather
than for its physical and emotional effects. Suffering lies in
the isolation of the Narrator from the social network that
sustains him and from the means of re-entry to it — money or
the ability to write. In the *Series* the Narrator considers
himself trapped and defined in the traditional *topos* of
madness, constantly and determinedly read in terms of its
symptoms and hence excluded from normal social intercourse
by his fellows even though he considers himself cured. The
conventional penitential mode which illness as theme
predicates is subverted. The *Complaint* has two distinct
thematic lines in consequence — it is a comedy in its
celebration of cure, and also a bewildered, but implicitly
accusatory, criticism of his friends. Patience and impatience
paradoxically interconnect in the poem.

Our expectation of a poem on mortality is partly fulfilled, for the Narrator tells his Friend that he has promised to translate a treatise on holy dying (*Dialogue* 205–31). The recollection of this project immediately introduces a further voice into the *Dialogue* as the Narrator embarks on a meditation upon mortality, arguing from the specifics of his own frailty:

'Of age am I fifty winter and thre;
Ripenesse of dethe / fast vpon me hastethe' (246–47)

to a collection of worn commonplaces on the transitory nature of earthly pleasure (260–94). The sudden introduction of a strikingly homely image of death emphasizes the conventional nature of this borrowed voice:

'Paleses / Maners / Castels grete & touris
Shal vs bireft be / by deeth þat ful sour is;
Shee is the rogh besom / which shal vs all
Sweepe out of this world / whan god list it fall.' (284–87)

The conventional list of symbols of earthly power limps to the forced rhyme and weakened semantics of the relative clause (*full sour is*) and thereby lends added force to the ensuing concretization of death as a *rogh besom* and the energy given by the enjambement to the line-head *sweepe*. The idea of Humankind as dust is strikingly defamiliarized by the image, throwing into relief the commonplaces of the rest of the passage.

But the project to translate *Learn to Die* is only partially linked to the mutability theme of the opening. It claims a prior existence to the *Complaint*, having been commissioned 'at the exitynge / and monicion / of a devout man' (234–35), and therefore continues the social reference. Devotionally, it is offered in part as an act of penance by the Narrator in gratitude for his cure (211–17), but the announcement follows upon his intemperate attack on false moneyers, and the first reason offered for the translation is that it will restrain men from vice. As with the *Complaint*, penitence and attack join together in the proposal. But the defiant defence by the narrator of his restoration to health now also seems contradicted by his self-construction as an example of human infirmity ('More am I heuy now vp-on a day' [253]), which understandably elicits a response of concern and caution from the Friend, who sees in this admission further evidence of his continuing illness. The juxtaposition of the two voices suggests symptomatically significant swings of mood.

The execution of the project also raises difficulties. The narrator states that it will be his last work:

'And whan that endyd is / I nevar thinke,
more in englyshe aftar / be occupied;' (239–40)

but the subsequent development of the *Series* reduces this sad claim to rhetorical gesture. This translation is deferred to introduce the tale of *Jereslaus' Wife*. Offered in 'penance' for the Narrator's alleged dispraise of women and dedicated to their honour, it ironically offsets the penitential nature of the subsequent *Learn to Die*. And although the Narrator claims that his warning of mortality was intended as the final voice in the *Series*, presumably in fulfilment of his intention to make it his final work, it yields that significant position to the tale of *Jonathas*, at his Friend's request. The fiction of social relationships serves to determine the content and structure of the *Series*.

Commissioners and Consumers

The ability to read people and texts appropriately is central to the progression of the *Series*. As it unfolds, it reveals the power of the reader, reflected in those who know the Narrator and his poems — his friends in general and the Friend in particular. These characters become destabilizing

devices within the *Series*, agents who disrupt the progress of
the programme envisaged by its Narrator. As 'consumers' of
poetry and as 'readers' of the Narrator himself they also
establish the social dimension of the work. David Greetham
suggests that Hoccleve has:

> brought this frame device into the centre of the poem, placing
> the stories on the periphery of the work. The *Series* is,
> structurally, *The Canterbury Tales* inside out.
>
> (1988-89, 247)[6]

The audience emerges as the true begetter of both the Narrator
and his poems.

The Narrator's dilemma throughout lies in his inability to
determine the response of others to him or to his work. He
sees friendship as a form of power that can require
unquestioning credence from his reader regardless of what he
says:

> 'A verray freend yeueth credence & feith
> Vn-to his freend / what so he speke & wryte.'
>
> (*Dialogue* 332–33)

Although the theme of friendship is not explicitly developed,
allusions to Cicero's *De Amicitia*, to Solomon and to
'[a]uctoritees an heep' (360) draw attention to the familiar
theme, and perhaps recall that supine acquiescence in a
friend's opinion is not there commended.[7] Not surprisingly,
the Narrator cannot claim this credence and finds his work

---

[6] See also John Burrow, *Ricardian Poetry* (1971, 51), where he claims
that the *Complaint* and *Dialogue* make the narratives from the *Gesta
Romanorum* 'appear remote and fantastic'.

[7] Although Cicero commends constancy in friendship in *De Amicitia*,
cap. 18, he also says in cap. 24 that to admonish and be admonished, and
to accept advice without resentment is also a part of friendship (ed. Falconer
1923, 174–77, 196–99).

misunderstood and himself misread (as he sees it) by his friends in the *Complaint*. Friendship and betrayal are major themes in both *Jereslaus' Wife* and *Jonathas*.

The genesis of the *Complaint* and of *Jereslaus' Wife* are comparable. The Narrator embarks upon the tale to regain the favour of women who, he has been told, have been offended by his earlier *Letter of Cupid*. He protests that he was a mere translator and cannot be held responsible for the words of another ('I nas in þat cas / but a reportour' *Dialogue* 761), but then goes on to marvel at one who would misinterpret his work:

> 'He mis-auysed is / and eek to blame.
> Whan I it spak / I spak conpleynyngly;
> I to hem thoghte no repreef ne shame.
> What world is this / how vndirstande am I?
> Looke in the same book / what stikith by?' (771–75)

'How am I understood?' Women have misread the text and, seeing it as mediating between author and reader, have constructed its author as a mysogynist. Their 'text', as reported by the Friend, has become more powerful than the work itself. The Friend utters it as truth: '… in thepistle of Cupyde / Thow haast of hem / … largeliche said' (*Dialogue* 754–55). He believes it even though, as he later admits, he has never read the *Letter* (781). But his report of the work's reception by women readers has the power to compel the Narrator to penance and to divert him from his intended programme. He now offers *Jereslaus' Wife* as penance to purge his guilt and to demonstrate the honour in which he holds women.

The Narrator similarly presents himself as a misunderstood text. His inability to control the interpretation of the *Letter of Cupid* by the reader is analogous to his inability to control the way others regard him, as he has already sadly recognized:

I may not lett a man / to ymagine
ferre above the mone / yf that hym lyst;
there-by the sowthe / he may not determyn[e].

(Complaint 197–99)

Others are misreading him in the light of the text of *wyld infirmytie* (40) from the past.

 Though the Narrator seeks to elude the conventional language of illness, it is within that language that his colleagues confine him. From his situation, it is the world that is alienated from him, not vice-versa: 'the worlde me made a straunge continance' (*Complaint* 70). Doob has shown that the comments attributed to his friends collectively correspond to the standard symptoms of madness as described by Bartholomeus Anglicus and goes on to argue that the conventional character of the symptoms should make us hesitate to propose that the narrator's illness reflects an illness suffered by the historical Hoccleve (1974, 221, 226). The point is rather that the Narrator's friends approach him through a diagnostic vocabulary derived from medical treatises and define and imprison him — and themselves — in their discourse. There is, finally, no language of 'normality' which the Narrator can substitute for that discourse; he can only offer a discourse which constructs him as an *exemplum* not of madness but of patience, which he must defend against the alternative, preferred by his Friend, the abandonment of discourse:

'reherse thow it not / ne it a-wake;
… for I can not finde
O man to speake of it …' (*Dialogue* 27, 32–33)

First, however, the Narrator scans himself to see if his meaning can be made clearer. The mirror-episode in the *Complaint* has been discussed as a pathetic and naturalistic scene, but the mirror also serves the Narrator as a text which he seeks to read as others read it, and which he tries to emend, replacing his habitual expressions by one that he believes will reflect his inner normality and be so read by those around:

> 'this countinance, I am svre, and this chere,
> If I forthe vse / is no thinge reprevable
> to them that have / conseytes resonable.' (166–68)

The episode literalizes the moral reference of the mirror as 'a model of good or virtuous conduct' and its literary application to books that supply such models (*mirour* MED sense 3). Hoccleve tellingly picks up the 'mirror' or *speculum* genre again in the *Dialogue* where the Narrator explains why it is unnecessary to translate Vegetius for the chivalrous Duke Humphrey;

> 'To cronicle his actes / wer a good deede,
> … it is a greet auauntage
> A man before him / to haue a mirour,
> Ther-in to see the path vn-to honour.' (603–9)

The denial underlines the fact that, in the process of rejecting the project, the Narrator admits the *speculum* genre into the *Series*, producing a mirror of Humphrey's acts in lines 561–616. The Friend subsequently offers the Narrator Geoffrey of Vinsauf's precept in similar terms (638–51):

> 'This may been vn-to thee / in thy makynge
> A good mirour …' (645–46)

But the mirror that the Narrator consults in his room is not metaphoric but optical; it reflects the Narrator's image back to him, with no 'accepted ideal' to which he should conform. How can he ensure that others read him as he intends? No more than he can ensure that readers understand his texts as he intends. 'How vndirstande am I?' applies to text and Narrator alike.

An ostensible consequence of the *Complaint* is the Narrator's final acceptance of consolation and patience in stoical indifference to the world. But this pose of resignation is subsequently undercut. The reactive and vulnerable character of the Narrator, deflected from his aims by the desire to meet the changing expectations of his readership, is the device by which the progress of the *Series* is randomized. He repeatedly surrenders control of his work to others. Though his Prologue points logically to a meditation upon mortality, he claims his translation of *Learn to Die*, as we saw earlier, to be 'at the exitynge / and monicion / of a devout man' (*Dialogue* 234–35). Of his intended commission to Duke Humphrey he appeals to his Friend:

> 'Now, good freend / shoue at the cart, I yow preye;
> What thyng may I make vn-to his plesance?
> Withouten your reed / noot I what to seye.'
>
> (*Dialogue* 617–19)

The pleading voice behind the colloquialism contrasts with the earlier determined defence of the *Complaint* against the Friend's objections. The Narrator seeks to mould his text and himself still to the conceptions of others. The Friend's advice, to regain the favour of his women-readers, returns the Narrator to the concerns about the reception of his work and the consequences to himself:

> 'ffor looth me were / thow sholdest aght wryte
> Wherthurgh / thow mightest gete any maugree;' (794–95)

and it is the Friend who passes final judgement and determines the story's final voice, the prose moralization:

> And to this moralyzynge I me spedde,
> In prose wrytynge it / hoomly and pleyn,
> ffor he conseillid me / do so / certeyn.
>
> (*Jereslaus' Wife: Epilogue* 24–26)

The effect of the addition is to set out plainly (*hoomly and pleyn*) the way in which the tale is to be read. It moves the tale from a romance of separation and restoration, as the

Narrator had significantly left it, into the closed genre of
exemplum. How dead that term *moralyzynge* sounds! The
Narrator complies with comic speed (*I me spedde*) and the
same apparent helplessness with which he sought advice on
the choice of subject.

A similar abnegation of responsibility occurs at the end
of the *Joys of Heaven*:

> This booke thus to han endid had y thoght,
> But my freend made me change my cast;
> Cleene out of þat purpos hath he me broght.
> *(Jonathas: Prologue* 1–3)

As the Narrator recognizes, the Friend's demands are
inconsistent. Initially he advised the Narrator to win the favour
of women by a story of womanly patience triumphant; now he
seeks a cautionary tale about a covetous woman. The two tales
are designed for two specific readers, Duke Humphrey and the
Friend's son, but evoke two different genres, praise and censure of women. The Narrator foresees the way that he will
now be constructed:

> ... 'o, beholde & see
> The double man / o, yondir, lo, gooth he
> That hony first yaf / and now yeueth galle:' (39–41)

which challenges the Friend's earlier reassurance that he
advises him in his own interests (*Dialogue* 794–95). At a
referential level, Hoccleve points to the problems of satisfying
a readership of diverse needs and expectations, the poet as the
slave to the market who loses his own integrity and voice in
the process of pleasing others. At a structural level, the Friend
becomes the means of randomizing the work and deferring its
closure.

Ironically, by juxtaposing these two ostensibly
contradictory genres at the Friend's request, the Narrator re-
emphasizes his vulnerability to the interpretations of women
readers — such as Karen A. Winstead (1993), who makes the

valid point that the two genres are mutually reflective and complementary in this context. The role of victim to male oppression occupied by Jereslaus' Wife is a consequence of her own faulty judgement when in authority: she proves a bad 'reader' of others. Her subsequent patience in adversity and her defence of her marital chastity can then be read as stereotypical female virtues that confirm her subservient position in a male-dominated hierarchy. 'Whereas [*Jereslaus's Wife*] fails to disprove antifeminist stereotypes, *Jonathas* explicitly confirms them.' (Winstead 1993, 150) The ambivalent potential of the *Letter of Cupid* is realized again.

The full irony of this concern with the response of the female readership becomes evident at the end of the *Series* when the final *envoi* (p. 242) discloses the work as a deconstruction of the petitionary poem and the petitionary poet. The dedication to a woman, 'my lady / of Westmerland', half-aunt to Duke Humphrey, has behind it these earlier insecurities about the potentially 'misguided' response of women readers which are reflected in the injunction to the text '[t]o plese hir wommanhede / do thy might'. Having exposed the processes of its own construction, the text seeks the patron-reader's informed understanding, making obsequious appeal to her 'noble excellence' and 'nobleye' for the acceptance of the work and its male author.

In this way, the work is redefined as an act of communication which confirms the social hierarchy of patron and poet ('[h]ir humble seruant', 'byseeche hire') and pleads for acceptance ('[t]hee to receyue'). This request for acceptance similarly gains force from what has gone before, the social alienation of the Narrator. Hence, in accepting the various discourses as a single 'smal book', the patron acknowledges the author of the work and becomes a point both of closure and also of potential reintegration. The poem thus finally affirms the social and interpretative authority of the reader.[8]

Currencies of Communication

Within the structure of the *Series*, Hoccleve is able to redirect the familiar opposition of *experience* and *auctorite*. In Chaucer books speak to the present with the wisdom of the past:

> For out of olde feldes, as men seyth,
> Cometh al this newe corn from yer to yere,
> And out of olde bokes, in good feyth,
> Cometh al this newe science that men lere.
>
> (*The Parliament of Fowls*, 22–25)

A line of transmission is made explicit here, one which shapes our perceptions of past and of present in ways whose reliability is affirmed by nothing more than its manuscript transmission. Books beget books, and authors become the seminal agents of that generation. Hoccleve, as James Simpson has perceptively demonstrated, 'points insistently to the textuality of his work' (1991, 16), but we are more conscious of the book or manuscript as a token of social exchange than as a repository of past wisdom. The focus remains upon the diversity of discourse. As texts, books contain the various registers accepted by society; as objects, they are part of the currency that enables relationships within society.[9] Books belong to and are shared among people. They are passed

---

[8] Winstead suggests, however, that 'in dedicating the Durham manuscript to Lady Westmorland, Hoccleve intended an oblique criticism of the countess.' (1993, 152)

[9] This develops John Burrow's comment that: '[i]n the world of Hoccleve's *Series*, books are part of life — patrons commission them, readers borrow them, authors worry about them.' (1984, 270)

among friends for edification (*Dialogue* 309–78); translated as
a favour in response to a friend's request (*Dialogue* 232–38;
Jonathas: Prologue 1–7); and augmented with a moral, also
at a friend's request (*Jereslaus' Wife: Epilogue* 1–28). They
are commissioned by patrons (*Dialogue* 526–38), dedicated to
them (*Series: Envoi*); and serve as petitions for money to them
(e.g. *La Male Regle* 409–48). When Hoccleve utters his
Complaint, it manifests itself in the form of a manuscript that
is submitted to a friend's critical judgement. Books represent
an essential component of his 'social network', components of
a dialogue; where they come from matters less than the
relationships of equality and of hierarchy that they signal and
cement.

Hoccleve's social commodification of the text has a
counterpart in the frequently noted concern in his poems with
money. Many of Hoccleve's poems petition for due payment.
The book is not proposed as a purchasable commodity, but as
a token of a writer's esteem which a noble patron should
reciprocate by the gift of money.[10] The direct plea for money
is both a genre and a device of closure. As the voice of
consolation provides the conventional ending to the
Complaint, so the petition for money provides the ostensibly
conventional purpose of and closure to *La Male Regle*,
drawing us back to the book as a means of re-establishing
social hierarchy and esteem. The latter work provides a useful
basis for approaching the *Complaint*. Money and texts are
inextricably linked. Ostensibly the Narrator has squandered
money on social pleasure, buying drinks for girls, paying
promptly and lavishly to cooks and tavern-keepers, hiring
boats from the appreciative Thames ferrymen. But in fact what
he has bought is words:

> To suffre hem paie, had been no courtesie: (151)

---

[10] On the petitionary poem, see John Burrow (1981).

Wher was a gretter maister eek than y, (177)

Wherfore I was the welcomere algate,
And for 'a verray gentil man' y-holde. (183–84)

Othir than 'maistir'/ callid was I neuere. (201)

The oral text here is a token of exchange as much as the
written. But the words which signify so much to the narrator
— *courtesie*, *gentil*, *maistir* — have, on the lips of the street
traders, been drained of their overtones of moral worth and
social dignity. As he realizes, they do not have the inherent
value that he assigned to them. But the realization that

> Right so the feyned wordes of plesance
> Annoyen aftir / thogh they plese a tyme
> To hem þat been vnwyse of gouernance, (241–43)

raises the question of how *wordes of plesance* are to be
recognized as *feyned*. Is the petitionary poem merely an
extension of the tradesman's obsequiousness? Hoccleve returns
to this important issue of verification in the *Complaint*; and
not only his own words, but also those of his fellow-clerks
who support his claim to be cured, are suspect (299–301).

In context, the sudden and violent attack upon those who
debase the coinage (*Dialogue* 99–198) can be seen not only as
an example of contemporary social reference but also as an
extension of the Narrator's concern with the validity of
language. The passage has its origins in the passing comment
that being ill is not like being:

> '… for an homysede yknowe,
> or an extorcioner / or a robbowr,
> or for a coin clypper …' (64–66).

The comment is made in the wider context of praise for God
who has cured the Narrator, a praise which culminates in
92–98:

'his vysytacion is a spectacle
in whiche that I / beholde may and se,
bet then I dyd / how great a lorde is he.' (96–98)

Like the paraphrase of the book in the *Complaint*, but with
even greater disjunctive force, the attack on false coiners is
marked off from what precedes and follows. Again, there is no
syntactic linkage but also no ostensible logical connection:

'but, frind, amonge the vises that right now
rehersed I, one of them, dare I saye,
hathe hurt me sore ...': (99–101)

but marks a total change of direction, and with it a shift to a
more conversational movement and tone from the preceding
praise of God. Its self-focus and tone of indignation (*rehersed
I*, *dare I*, *hurt me*), is sustained in the rhetorical questions
(106–7, 120–24, 148–49) and in the general violence of the
language and length of the complaint. The account ends as
abruptly as it started, suddenly drawing in the *frinde* and
apologetically acknowledging the attack as a lengthy
digression:

'lo, frinde / nowe haue I myne entent vnreke
of my longe tale / displese yow nowght.' (197–98)

The theme has taken root and bursts out at length and force
without regard to context. The Friend seems tactfully to ignore
the outburst and reverts to the *Complaint*. The passage is, on
the surface, another well-defined voice, an example of
venality-complaint, urging social reform in a personalized
protest. But its intrusion both disrupts the sense of the *Series*
as an ordered structure and challenges the restoration of the
Narrator to mental balance. Juxtaposed with the praise of God,
this bathetic descent calls into question the assurances of
patience given previously and in so doing implicitly analogizes
the value of words and the value of money.

The social value of the book in Hoccleve complicates the way in which intertextuality works within the poems. A most revealing example is the book from which he derives consolation in the *Complaint*. The account is set off structurally within the poem. Again, it opens abruptly, without syntactic connection to what has gone before:

> This othar day / a lamentacion
> of a wofull man / in a boke I sye, (309–10)

and closes surprisingly by offering a casual and therefore naturalistic reason for his concentration only upon the *lamentacion*:

> lenger I thowght[e] / red have in this boke,
> but so it shope / that I ne myght[e] nowght;
> he that it owght / agayne it to hym toke,
> me of his haste vnware … (372–75)

Thanks to A.G. Rigg (1970) we know that the book to which Hoccleve is referring was Isidore of Seville's *Synonyma*; but the significance of the text resides in the Narrator's identification with the sufferer and the acceptance of language and theme, not in the authority of the book and its author. *Reason* provides from its pages the conventional wisdom of patience and resignation and provides the model for the closure of resignation in the *Complaint* at lines 379–413. The genre also offers the Narrator a conventional personal paradigm and directs the poem to a recognizable and acceptable exemplary conclusion.

Moreover, the borrowed book speaks with a different, 'literary' voice from the more 'colloquial' register of the Narrator, even when handling the same subject; compare:

> This troubly lyfe / hathe all to longe enduryd,
> not have I wyst / how in my skynne to turne; (302–3)

with

> Gretar plesaunce / were it me to dye,

by many folde / than for to lyve soo;
sorows so many / in me multiplye,
that my lyfe is / to me a wery foo. (330–33)

The compression of *this troubly lyfe* and the concrete colloquialism of *in my skynne to turne* throw into relief the tired images (*sorows ... multiplye*; *lyfe ... a ... foo*), weak phrases (*gretar plesaunce, by many folde*) and leisurely syntax of 330–33. Simpson has rightly pointed out that an appeal to another 'external' book in general strengthens our sense that the rest of the text is 'non-literary' (1991, 20). But the change of stylistic register also contributes to that impression. Lillian Feder protests that the *Complaint* is the work of: 'a poet whose efforts at self-examination are finally blocked by a prescribed moral conclusion' (1980, 109). But this 'book-style' heightens the sense of individual anguish caught in the preceding colloquial and particularized account, which remains the dominant effect for the reader.

And the borrowed book also has a social value, because the Narrator came by it through the kindness of a friend. Rigg believes that the idea of a loan from a friend which was then recalled is an abridging fiction on Hoccleve's part which was suggested to him by the alleged circumstances in which Isidore was led to compose his work, the chance finding of a copy of Cicero's *Synonyma* (1970, 573). The circumstances under which the book was acquired further complicate our reading by challenging the alienation of which the Narrator protests. Moreover, the intervention of the friend to reclaim his book when only partly read is the first example in the *Series* of the disjunctive function that the device of 'friend' serves within the overall structure. The friend speaks to him through the book but also offers to him the philosophy which can restore him to peace with himself and the generic model which his discourse should emulate.

Conclusion

Although it is usually compared with the *Canterbury Tales*, the *Series* would perhaps be more revealingly compared with the *House of Fame* in its concern with the extent to which we are defined by the discourse of others and controlled by their expectations.[11] Hoccleve proves by his quotations, allusions and themes that he is well aware of the traditions against which he reacts. The abrupt changes in local style and overall direction call into question the implicit certainties of art that Bennett seems to require when he complains of Hoccleve's inability 'to control or refine his matter in a clear picture' (1947, 149). Today, perhaps, we can derive greater pleasure from the sophistication of the naive in the work. The confident arbitrariness of the *Series* and the ironic way in which registers and genres comment upon each other distinguish Hoccleve as a major exponent of 'the tradition of anti-tradition'.

---

[11] Both Chaucer in *The House of Fame* and Hoccleve resist the idea that the 'self' is publicly definable; compare *HF* 1876–78: 'Sufficeth me, as I were ded, / That no wight have my name in honde. / I wot myself best how I stonde;' with Hoccleve, *Dialogue* 477–79: 'ffreend, as to þat, he lyueth nat þat can / Knowe / how it standith with an othir wight, / So wel as him self'.

Bibliography

THE following abbreviations are used:

CUP   Cambridge University Press
EETS The Early English Text Society
e.s.   extra series
MED *Middle English Dictionary*, edited by Hans Kurath *et al.* (Ann Arbor: University of Michigan Press, 1956–).
o.s.   original series
OUP   Oxford University Press

Editions

Biblia Pauperum:
Henry (1987) *The Biblia Pauperum*, edited by Avril Henry (Aldershot: Scolar Press).

Blamires (1992) *Woman Defamed and Woman Defended: An Anthology of Medieval Texts*, edited by Alcuin Blamires with Karen Pratt and C.W. Marx (Oxford: Clarendon Press).

Bridget of Sweden:
Ellis (1987) *The 'Liber Celestis' of St Bridget of Sweden*, edited by Roger Ellis, Vol. 1, EETS o.s. 291 (Oxford: OUP).

Caxton, William:
Axon (1883) *The Game and Playe of the Chesse (1474)*,
    edited by William E. A. Axon (London: Eliot Stock).

Cessolis, Jacobus de:
Kopke (1879) *De Ludo Scacchorum*: *Mittheilungen aus dem
    Handschriften der Ritterakademie zu Brandenburg A.H.*,
    II, *Jacobus de Cessolis*, edited by Ernst Kopke
    (Brandenburg: Gustav Mathes).

Chaucer, Geoffrey:
Benson (1988) *The Riverside Chaucer*, 3rd edition, General
    Editor Larry D. Benson (Oxford: OUP).

Christine de Pizan:
Fenster and Erler (1990) *Epistre au dieu d'Amours*, in *Poems
    of Cupid, God of Love*, edited by Thelma S. Fenster and
    Mary Carpenter Erler (Leiden: E.J. Brill).

Roy (1891) *Oeuvres poétiques de Christine de Pisan*, II,
    edited by M. Roy (Paris: Firmin Didot).

Cicero:
Falconer (1923) Cicero: *De Senectute, De Amicitia, De
    Divinatione*, edited and translated by William Armistead
    Falconer. Loeb Classical Library (London: William
    Heinemann).

Guillaume de Deguileville:
Henry (1985–88) *The Pilgrimage of the Lyfe of the Manhode*,
    edited by Avril Henry, EETS o.s. 288 (1985); EETS o.s.
    292 (1988)(Oxford: OUP).

Foedera:

Thomas Rymer (1710) *Foedera, conventiones, literae, et cujuscunque generis acta publica inter Reges Angliae, et alios quosvis Imperatores, Reges, Pontifices, Principes, vel Communitates ...*, edited by Thomas Rymer. 20 vols: vol. 8 (London: A&J Churchill).

Thomas Rymer (1712) *Foedera*, vol. 9.

Hoccleve, Thomas:

Bowers (1992) The Ploughman's Tale in *The Canterbury Tales: Fifteenth-Century Continuations and Additions*, edited by John M. Bowers (Kalamazoo, MI: Medieval Institute Publications, Western Michigan University), pp. 23–32.

Fenster and Erler (1990) *The Letter of Cupid* in *Poems of Cupid, God of Love*, edited by Thelma S. Fenster and Mary Carpenter Erler (Leiden: E.J. Brill).

Furnivall (1970) *Hoccleve's Works* I *The Minor Poems in the Phillipps MS. 8151 (Cheltenham) and the Durham MS. III.9*, edited by Frederick J. Furnivall. EETS e.s. 61 (1892) (London: OUP). *Hoccleve's Works* II *The Minor Poems of the Ashburnham MS. Addit. 133*, edited by Sir Israel Gollancz EETS e.s. 73 (1925, for 1897) (London: OUP). Both reprinted in one volume (EETS 1937). Revised edition in one volume by Jerome Mitchell and A.I. Doyle, as *Hoccleve's Works: The Minor Poems*, EETS (London: OUP).

Furnivall (1897)   *Hoccleve's Works* III *The Regement of Princes and Fourteen Minor Poems*, edited by Frederick J. Furnivall, EETS e.s. 72 (London: Kegan Paul, Trench, Trübner and Co.).

O'Donoghue (1982)   *Thomas Hoccleve: Selected Poems*, edited by Bernard O'Donoghue (Manchester: Manchester University Press).

Seymour (1981)   *Selections from Hoccleve*, edited by M.C. Seymour (Oxford: Clarendon Press).

Lydgate, John:
Bergen (1906) *Lydgate's Troy Book*, Part I, edited by Henry Bergen, EETS e.s. 97 (London: OUP).

— (1908)   *Lydgate's Troy Book*, Part II, EETS e.s. 103 (London: OUP).

— (1910)   *Lydgate's Troy Book*, Part III, EETS e.s. 106 (London: OUP).

Le Roman de la Rose:
Horgan (1994)   *Guillaume de Lorris and Jean de Meun: The Romance of the Rose*, translated by Frances Horgan (Oxford: OUP).

Secretum Secretorum:
Manzalaoui (1977)   *Secretum Secretorum: Nine English Versions*, edited by M.A. Manzalaoui, EETS o.s. 276 (London: OUP).

Shepherd (1985)   *The Woman's Sharp Revenge: Five Women's Pamphlets from the Renaissance*, edited by S. Shepherd (London: Fourth Estate).

Facsimiles

Robinson (1982) *Manuscript Tanner 346: A Facsimile*, edited by Pamela R. Robinson (Norman: Pilgrim Books).

Secondary

Allen (1985) Prudence Allen, *The Concept of Woman: The Aristotelian Revolution 750 BC – AD 1250* (Montreal: Eden Press).

Allmand (1992)   Christopher Allmand, *Henry V* (London: Methuen).

d'Alverny (1977)   Marie-Thérèse d'Alverny, 'Comment les théologiens et les philosophes voient la femme', in *Cahiers de Civilisation Médiévale* 20, 105–29.

Aston (1984)   Margaret Aston, *Lollards and Reformers: Images and Literacy in Late Medieval Religion* (London: Hambledon).

Beer (1991) Jeanette Beer, 'Julius Caesar, Philip Augustus, and the Anonymous Translator of *Li Fet des Romains*' in *The Medieval Translator II*, edited by Roger Ellis, Westfield Publications in Medieval Studies V (London: Queen Mary and Westfield College), pp. 89–97.

Bennett (1947)   H.S. Bennett, *Chaucer and the Fifteenth Century* (Oxford: Clarendon Press).

Boffey (1994)   Julia Boffey, 'English Dream Poems of the Fifteenth Century and their French Connections', in *Literary Aspects of Courtly Culture: Selected Papers from the Seventh Triennial Congress of the International Courtly Literature Society, University of Massachusetts, Amherst, USA, 27 July – 1 August 1992*, edited by Donald Maddox and Sara Sturm-Maddox (Cambridge: D.S. Brewer), pp. 113–21.

Bornstein (1977)   Diane Bornstein, 'French Influence on Fifteenth-century English Prose as Exemplified by the Translation of Christine de Pisan's *Livre du corps de policie*', *Medieval Studies* 39, 369–86.

— (1981–82)   'Anti-Feminism in Thomas Hoccleve's Translation of Christine de Pizan's *Epistre au dieu d'amours*', *English Language Notes* 19, 7–14.

Bowers (1989a)   John M. Bowers, 'Hoccleve's Huntington Holographs: The First "Collected Poems" in English', *Fifteenth-Century Studies* 15, 27–51.

— (1989b)   'Hoccleve's Two Copies of *Lerne to Dye*: Implications for Textual Critics', *Papers of the Bibliographical Society of America* 83, 437–72.

Brewer (1978) *Chaucer: The Critical Heritage*, Vol. 1, edited by Derek Brewer (London: Routledge and Kegan Paul).

Bruins (1925)   J.G. Bruins, *Observations sur la langue d'Eustache Deschamps et de Christine de Pisan* (Amsterdam: De Dordrechtsche Drukkerij).

Burns (1993) E. Jane Burns, 'This Prick Which Is Not One: How Women Talk Back in Old French Fabliaux', in *Feminist Approaches to the Body in Medieval Literature*, edited by Linda Lomperis and Sarah Stanbury (Philadelphia: University of Pennsylvania Press), pp. 188–212.

Burrow (1971) J.A. Burrow, *Ricardian Poetry: Chaucer, Gower, Langland and the 'Gawain' Poet* (London: Routledge and Kegan Paul).

— (1981) 'The Poet as Petitioner', *Studies in the Age of Chaucer* 3, 61–75.

— (1984) 'Hoccleve's *Series*: Experience and Books', in *Fifteenth-Century Studies: Recent Essays*, edited by R.F. Yeager (Hamden, CT: Archon Books), pp. 259–73.

— (1994) *Thomas Hoccleve*. Authors of the Middle Ages 4. (Aldershot: Variorum).

Campbell (1925) P.G.C. Campbell, 'Christine de Pisan en Angleterre', *Revue de Littérature Comparée* 5, 659–70.

Clark (1982) Elizabeth A. Clark, *Jerome, Chrysostom, and Friends: essays and translations*, 2nd edition (New York: Edwin Mellen Press).

Classen (1990) Albrecht Classen, 'Love and Marriage in Late Medieval Verse: Oswald von Wolkenstein, Thomas Hoccleve and Michel Beheim', *Studia Neophilologica* 62, 163–88.

Doob (1974)   Penelope B.R. Doob, *Nebuchadnezzar's Children: Conventions of Madness in Middle English Literature* (New Haven: Yale University Press).

Edwards (1993) A.S.G. Edwards, 'The Chaucer Portraits in the Harley and Rosenbach Manuscripts', *English Manuscript Studies* 4, 268–71.

Ellis (1982)   Roger Ellis, '"Flores ad fabricandam ... coronam": An Investigation into the Uses of the Revelations of St Bridget of Sweden in Fifteenth-Century England', *Medium Ævum* 51, 163–86.

— (1986)   *Patterns of Religious Narrative in the 'Canterbury Tales'* (London: Croom Helm).

— (1992)   'Plain Speaking in Three Canterbury Tales', *Bulletin of the John Rylands Library* 74, 121–39.

Feder (1980) Lillian Feder, *Madness in Literature* (Princeton: Princeton University Press).

Ferster (1985)   Judith Ferster, *Chaucer on Interpretation* (Cambridge: CUP).

Field (1989) Rosalind Field, '*Ipomedon* to *Ipomadon A*: Two Views of Courtliness', in *The Medieval Translator: The Theory and Practice of Translation in the Middle Ages*, edited by Roger Ellis *et al.* (Cambridge: D.S. Brewer), pp. 135–41.

Fisher (1992)   John H. Fisher, 'A Language Policy for Lancastrian England', *PMLA* 107, 1168–80.

Fleming (1971) J.V. Fleming, 'Hoccleve's "Letter of Cupid" and the "Quarrel" over the *Roman de la Rose*', *Medium Ævum* 40, 21–40.

Fradenburg (1992) *Women and Sovereignty*, edited by Louise Olga Fradenburg (Edinburgh: Edinburgh University Press).

Goodman (1991) Jennifer Goodman, 'William Caxton and Anthony Woodville, Translators: the Case of the *Dictes and Sayengis of the Philosophres*', *New Comparison* 12, 7–22.

Greetham (1985) David Greetham, 'Normalisation of Accidentals in Middle English Texts: The Paradox of Thomas Hoccleve', *Studies in Bibliography* 38, 121–50.

— (1987) 'Challenges of Theory and Practice in the Editing of Hoccleve's *Regement of Princes*', in ed. Pearsall, *Manuscripts and Texts*, pp. 60–86.

— (1988–89) 'Self-Referential Artifacts; Hoccleve's Persona as a Literary Device', *Modern Philology* 86, 242–51.

Greg (1950–51) W.W. Greg, 'The Rationale of Copy-Text', *Studies in Bibliography* 3, 19–36.

Hagel (1984) Günter Hagel, *Thomas Hoccleve: Leben und Werk eines Schriftstellers im England des Spätmittelalters* (Frankfurt-am-Main: Lang).

Hammond (1969) Eleanor Prescott Hammond, *English Verse Between Chaucer and Surrey* (Durham, NC: Duke University Press, 1927; reprinted New York: Octagon Books).

Hanna (1992) Ralph Hanna III, 'Producing Manuscripts and Editions', in *Crux and Controversy in Middle English Textual Criticism*, edited by A.J. Minnis and Charlotte Brewer (Cambridge: D.S. Brewer), pp. 109–30.

Hansen (1992)   Elaine Tuttle Hansen, *Chaucer and the Fictions of Gender* (Berkeley: University of California Press).

Hasler (1990) Antony J. Hasler, 'Hoccleve's Unregimented Body', *Paragraph* 13, 164–83.

Heinrichs (1990) K. Heinrichs, *The Myths of Love: Classical Lovers in Medieval Literature* (University Park: Pennsylvania State University Press).

Jefferson (1987)   Judith A. Jefferson, 'The Hoccleve Holographs and Hoccleve's Metrical Practice', in Pearsall (1987), pp. 95–109.

Laidlaw (1982) J.C. Laidlaw, 'Christine de Pizan, the Earl of Salisbury and Henry IV', *French Studies* 36, 129–43.

Lawton (1985)   David Lawton, *Chaucer's Narrators* (Cambridge: D.S. Brewer).

— (1987) 'Dullness and the Fifteenth Century', *English Literary History* 54, 761–99.

Leicester (1990) H. Marshall Leicester, Jr, *The Disenchanted Self: Representing the Subject in the 'Canterbury Tales'* (Berkeley: University of California Press).

Lerer (1993) Seth Lerer, *Chaucer and His Readers: Imagining the Author in Late-Medieval England* (Princeton: Princeton University Press).

Loseff (1984) Lev Loseff, *On the Beneficence of Censorship: Aesopian Language in Modern Russian Literature*, translated by Jane Bobko (Munich: Otto Sagner).

McFarlane (1972) Kenneth B. McFarlane, *Lancastrian Kings and Lollard Knights* (Oxford: Clarendon Press).

Meale (1993) Carole M. Meale, '"… alle the bokes that I haue of latyn, englisch, and frensch": Laywomen and their Books in Late Medieval England', in *Women and Literature in Britain, 1150–1500*, edited by Carol M. Meale, Cambridge Studies in Medieval Literature, 17 (Cambridge: CUP), pp. 128–58.

Medcalf (1981) Stephen Medcalf, 'Inner and Outer' in *The Later Middle Ages*, edited by Stephen Medcalf (London: Methuen), pp. 123–40.

Minnis (1988) A.J. Minnis, *Medieval Theory of Authorship: Scholastic Literary Attitudes in the Later Middle Ages*, 2nd edition (Aldershot: Wildwood House).

Mitchell (1968) Jerome Mitchell, *Thomas Hoccleve: A Study in Early Fifteenth-Century English Poetic* (Urbana: University of Illinois Press).

Murphy (1994)   Colette Murphy, 'Lady Holy Church and Meed the Maid: Re-envisioning Female Personifications in *Piers Plowman*', in *Feminist Readings in Middle English Literature: The Wife of Bath and All Her Sect*, edited by Ruth Evans and Lesley Johnson (London: Routledge), pp. 140–64.

Nolan (1992)   Barbara Nolan, *Chaucer and the Tradition of the 'Roman Antique'*, Cambridge Studies in Medieval Literature, 15 (Cambridge: CUP).

Orme (1989)   Nicholas Orme, *Education and Society in Medieval and Renaissance England* (London: Hambledon).

Patterson (1989)   Lee Patterson, '"What Man Artow?": Authorial Self-Definition in *The Tale of Sir Thopas* and *The Tale of Melibee*', *Studies in the Age of Chaucer* 11, 117–75.

Pearsall (1977)   Derek Pearsall, *Old English and Middle English Poetry* (London: Routledge and Kegan Paul).

— (1987)   ed., *Manuscripts and Texts: Editorial Problems in Later Middle English Literature* (Cambridge: D.S. Brewer).

— (1992)   *The Life of Geoffrey Chaucer: A Critical Biography* (Oxford: Blackwell).

— (1994)   'Hoccleve's *Regement of Princes*: The Poetics of Royal Self-Representation', *Speculum* 69, 386–410.

Piper (1989)   A.J. Piper, unpublished notes to Durham, University Library MS Cosin V.ii.13. (deposited at Durham: Palace Green Library)

Quinn (1986–87) W.A. Quinn, 'Hoccleve's *Epistle of Cupid*', *The Explicator* 45, 7–10.

Richards (1995)   Earl Jeffrey Richards, 'In Search of a Feminist Patrology: Christine de Pizan and "les glorieux dotteurs" of the Church', *Mystics Quarterly* 21, 3–17.

Richardson (1985–86) Malcolm Richardson, 'Hoccleve in his Social Context', *Chaucer Review* 20, 313–22.

Rigg (1970) A.G. Rigg, 'Hoccleve's *Complaint* and Isidore of Seville', *Speculum* 45, 564–74.

Scanlon (1990)   Larry Scanlon, 'The King's Two Voices: Narrative and Power in Hoccleve's *Regement of Princes*', in *Literary Practice and Social Change in Britain, 1380–1530*, edited by Lee Patterson (Berkeley: University of California Press), pp. 216–47.

— (1994) *Narrative, Authority, and Power: The Medieval Exemplum and the Chaucerian Tradition*, Cambridge Studies in Medieval Literature, 20 (Cambridge: CUP).

Schulz (1937)   H.C. Schulz, 'Thomas Hoccleve, Scribe', *Speculum* 12, 71–81.

Scott (1989) Joan W. Scott, 'Gender: A Useful Category of Historical Analysis', in *Coming To Terms: Feminism, Theory, Politics*, edited by Elizabeth Weed (London: Routledge), pp. 81–100.

Seymour (1974)   M.C. Seymour, 'The Manuscripts of Hoccleve's *Regiment of Princes*', *Edinburgh Bibliographical Society Transactions*, vol. iv, pt 7, 255–97.

— (1975)   Introduction to *On the Properties of Things: John Trevisa's Translation of Bartholomæus Anglicus De Proprietatibus Rerum: A Critical Text*. Vol. I (Oxford: Clarendon Press).

Simpson (1991)   James Simpson, 'Madness and Texts: Hoccleve's *Series*', in *Chaucer and Fifteenth-Century Poetry*, edited by Julia Boffey and Janet Cowen, King's College London Medieval Studies, 5 (London: King's College), pp. 15–29.

— (1995)   'Nobody's Man: Thomas Hoccleve's *Regement of Princes*', in *London and Europe in the Later Middle Ages*, edited by Julia Boffey and Pamela King, Westfield Publications in Medieval Studies, 9 (London: Queen Mary and Westfield College), pp. 149–80.

Smith (1900)   G. Gregory Smith, *The Transition Period* (Edinburgh and London: Blackwood).

Spearing (1985) A.C. Spearing, *Medieval to Renaissance in English Poetry* (Cambridge: CUP).

Strohm (1992)   Paul Strohm, 'Queens as Intercessors', in *Hochon's Arrow. The Social Imagination of Fourteenth-Century Texts* (Princeton: Princeton University Press), pp. 95–119.

Tanselle (1989) G. Thomas Tanselle, *A Rationale of Textual Criticism* (Philadelphia: University of Pennsylvania Press).

ten Brink (1893) Bernhard ten Brink, *History of English Literature*, Vol. 2, translated by William Clarke Robinson (London: G. Bell & Sons).

Thornley (1967) Eva M. Thornley, 'The Middle English Penitential Lyric and Hoccleve's Autobiographical Poetry', *Neuphilologische Mitteilungen* 68, 295–321.

Thundy (1979) Zacharias P. Thundy, 'Matheolus, Chaucer, and the Wife of Bath', in *Chaucerian Problems and Perspectives: Essays Presented to Paul E. Beichner*, edited by Edward Vasta and Zacharias P. Thundy (Notre Dame, IN: University of Notre Dame Press), pp. 24–58.

Torti (1989) Anna Torti, 'From "History" to "Tragedy": The Story of Troilus and Criseyde in Lydgate's *Troy Book* and Henryson's *Testament of Cresseid*', in *The European Tragedy of Troilus*, edited by Piero Boitani (Oxford: Clarendon Press), pp. 171–97.

— (1991) *The Glass of Form: Mirroring Structures from Chaucer to Skelton* (Cambridge: D.S.Brewer).

— (1992) 'Hoccleve's Attitude Towards Women: "I shoop me do my peyne and diligence To wynne hir loue by obedience"', in *A Wyf Ther Was: Essays in Honour of Paule Mertens-Fonck*, edited by Juliette Dor (Liège: Université de Liège), pp. 264–74.

Waller (1978) M.S. Waller, 'Christine de Pisan's *Epistle of the God of Love* and the Medieval Image of Woman', *Christianity and Literature* 27, 41–52.

Willard (1984) Charity Cannon Willard, *Christine de Pizan: Her Life and Works: A Biography* (New York: Persea Books).

Winstead (1993) Karen A. Winstead, '"I am al othir to yow than yee weene": Hoccleve, Women, and the *Series*', *Philological Quarterly* 72, 143–55.

Index

Manuscripts mentioned in the text

(Burrow 1994, 50–54, contains a full listing of the extant MSS of Hoccleve's works)

Geoffrey Chaucer
  The Canterbury Tales:
    Aberystwyth, National
    Library of Wales
      Peniarth 392D (Hengwrt)
    San Marino, CA,
    Huntington Library
      EL 26.C.9 (Ellesmere)

Thomas Hoccleve
  The Regiment of Princes:
    Cambridge
      Corpus Christi College
      496
      University Library
      Hh.iv.11
    London
      British Library
      Arundel 38
      Harley 4866
      Harley 7333
      Royal 17.D.vi
      Society of Antiquaries
      134
    Philadelphia, PA,
      Rosenbach Museum &
      Library
      1083/30

The Series:
  Durham University
  Library
    Cosin V.iii.9

Collected Shorter Poems:
  San Marino, CA,
  Huntington Library
    HM 111
    HM 744

The Letter of Cupid:
  Oxford, Bodleian Library
    Tanner 346
    Fairfax 16
  Durham University
  Library
    Cosin V.ii.13

The Miracle of the Virgin / The
Ploughman's Tale:
  Oxford
    Christ Church 152

The Formulary:
  London, British Library
    Additional 24062

General Index